# MICRO
# FOOD
# GARDENING

Inspiring | Educating | Creating | Entertaining

Brimming with creative inspiration, how-to projects, and useful information to enrich your everyday life, Quarto Knows is a favorite destination for those pursuing their interests and passions. Visit our site and dig deeper with our books into your area of interest: Quarto Creates, Quarto Cooks, Quarto Homes, Quarto Lives, Quarto Drives, Quarto Explores, Quarto Gifts, or Quarto Kids.

First Published in 2021 by Cool Springs Press, an imprint of The Quarto Group, 100 Cummings Center, Suite 265-D, Beverly, MA 01915, USA.
T (978) 282-9590 F (978) 283-2742 QuartoKnows.com

Cool Springs Press titles are also available at discount for retail, wholesale, promotional, and bulk purchase. For details, contact the Special Sales Manager by email at specialsales@quarto.com or by mail at The Quarto Group, Attn: Special Sales Manager, 100 Cummings Center, Suite 265-D, Beverly, MA 01915, USA.

25 24 23 22 21          1 2 3 4 5

ISBN: 978-0-7603-6983-8

Digital edition published in 2021

Library of Congress Cataloging-in-Publication Data available

Design: Megan Jones Design
Cover Image: Jen McGuinness
Page Layout: Megan Jones Design
Photography: Jen and Rob McGuinness, except shutterstock on page 52

Printed in China

# MICRO FOOD GARDENING

## Project Plans and Plants for Growing Fruits and Veggies in Tiny Spaces

Jen McGuinness

COOL
SPRINGS
PRESS

# CONTENTS

◇◇◇◇◇◇

◁ Repurposing items, such as this bicycle basket, can make for fun and creative ways to grow edibles in small spaces.

# INTRODUCTION

# WHY GROW MICRO FOOD?

Growing up in a two-family home in Queens, New York, meant space was always at a premium. Being in the city, pavement was the norm—including porches, patios, and driveways (if you were lucky enough to have one). Tall apartment buildings nearby meant limited sunlight, making one side of our home the desirable sunny window space for plants. That isn't to say that there weren't any gardens, but they were often on the smaller side—such as a postage stamp front yard or a stoop to put containers on. That meant if you wanted to grow food, you needed to get creative with the available space. My grandfather set an example for me early on as he continually found inventive ways to grow the food he wanted.

Today, we have so many more options for growing food, including varieties bred for small spaces and light fixtures to correct our dark spaces. But there is still one thing that can elude us—and that is available space to grow in.

That's how micro food gardening is different than raised bed gardening or container gardening. Micro food gardening focuses on plants that stay very compact—so you'll be able to grow edibles even if you only have a front porch, window box, or windowsill. Not only is it fun to select petite varieties of plants to grow, but it is also enjoyable discovering container options for display.

Growing food in smaller spaces is a trend that is not going away. It's estimated that 68% of the world population will be living in cities by 2050, according to the World Economic Forum.

In order to accommodate a growing population, space will continue to be at a premium. A lack of land does not mean you cannot grow any food. As you'll see in this book, there are many compact projects that will allow you to grow edibles in a limited space.

◀ Edible pea shoots can be grown
in decorative mason jars.

# THE WORLD OF MICRO EDIBLES

The popularity and passion of growing your own food is noticeable through social media posts and buying trends at garden centers. Plant breeders have observed the need to grow plants in smaller spaces, and as a result, we now have many compact and dwarf edible varieties to choose from when planning what we want to grow. Whether you live in an apartment, condo, or a small home, there is a plant to fit your space. Even if you do not live in a city, suburban areas are also finding innovative ways to adapt to smaller spaces—meaning it is time to get creative in using patios, decks, stoops, and balconies!

## WHAT IS CONSIDERED A MICRO VEGGIE, FRUIT, OR HERB?

Generally speaking, it is any plant that is approximately 18 inches (46 cm) or smaller when the plant has reached harvest size. Some plants, such as vines, may grow a little larger but still produce minisize fruits. Veggies, fruits, and herbs all offer an edible component, which makes them different than a plant considered *ornamental*, which does not feature any edible parts. There are even some micro edible flowers, which can add a splash of color to salads, ice cubes, and cakes.

Seed catalogs offer the best selection of mini plants to grow. You can grow mini tomato plants, leafy veggies, sprouts, microgreens, and more. When reviewing seed packets or catalog descriptions, look for "does well in containers"—and then check the plant's height and spread. If you are not ready to start growing your own plants from seeds, you might be able to request micro plant varieties from your independent garden center as well.

Throughout the book, you will find recommended plants to use with each project, along with plant profiles and growing advice. This will help you choose the best project (or projects!)

Dwarf vegetable varieties, like this eggplant, can be considered micro when they max out at 18 inches (46 cm) tall.

Edible flowers such as these violas offer a splash of color to your micro food garden.

to suit your space. Once you figure out what you want to grow, you'll need to pick the container it will grow in. (See page 18 for more information on different types of containers.) Many of the projects featured in this book include objects you may not have considered as containers before—including repurposing items you might have in your home to grow food. The projects can be adapted to fit the space you have, and you will find that you do not need a ton of space to grow edibles. There are even ways to build items that can serve a useful purpose in your space, such as a compact worm bin and a rain barrel (don't worry, I'll show you how!).

## THE BENEFITS OF MICRO FOOD GARDENING

Micro edibles need to not only provide food, but look good, too. If you are new to gardening, many of the projects in this book provide an opportunity to experiment with growing plants. Be careful—once you try your first homegrown tomato, you might be hooked! Many of the projects are themed around the delicious meals you can make with your micro edibles, such as the Salsa Garden, Stir-Fry Garden, and Omelet Combo.

Growing micro edibles allows you to garden on your schedule—that might be from home, taking care of kids, or spending time in an office

Decorative head planters not only take up little space, but are whimsical options for growing edibles, such as these chives.

for 10–12 hours a day. Many of the projects can be assembled in a few hours or over a weekend. Then, you just have to take care of the plants you are growing. I've divided the projects in the book into cool season and warm season projects, so you will find a project suitable for the season you are in. In addition, many of the indoor projects can also be started at any time of year.

Growing micro food is a great way to get children interested in gardening as well. Projects in this book can be family activities (such as the Muffin Pan Basil and Edible Flowers projects) that encourage hands-on learning and patience. Not only can growing edibles lead to a sense of accomplishment in children, but they are exposed to different types of food that they might not normally eat, which could lead to healthy eating habits in the future.

As you'll see in the next section, you can assess your growing conditions and have some control over soil mix, watering, and placement. I can't wait to share with you ways to grow micro food in small spaces. I'm excited to get started—and I hope you are, too.

You can grow many micro varieties of vegetables, such as tomatoes, eggplants, and peppers, from seed.

# SETTING UP YOUR SPACE

When it comes to growing your own micro food, you don't need a dedicated room in your home or apartment. Many of the projects in this book can be done outside on a porch, patio, or stoop; or on a table, kitchen counter, or windowsill indoors.

To keep your plants happy, you will need to give them the light they need, water for hydration, and nutritious soil to feed their roots. When thinking of your ideal growing space, consider the following for indoor and outdoor locations.

## ASSESSING YOUR OUTDOOR SPACE

Take a look at the space you have available and make some notes. Look for an area on your porch, patio, or balcony that will be protected from intense rainfall (including runoff from rain gutters) and sheltered from heavy winds in storms. If you rent, will your landlord allow you to drill holes into the walls or siding for a trellis or allow you to hang a window box from your balcony? Make notes on how much sunlight your spot gets a day. (See page 21 for more on lighting.) Taking into account the answers to your questions above, you can see which projects are possible in your space.

## ASSESSING YOUR INDOOR SPACE

When finding a spot indoors to grow your micro food, choose a spot protected from pets. This is to keep them from sampling your plant or knocking the container—and plant—over. Are you planning to grow your edibles in a sunny window or will you need a grow light to brighten your space? Good houseplant etiquette also applies to growing micro food indoors. You'll want to place plants away from window or air-conditioning drafts and protect plants from dry, intense radiator heat.

◄ Micro food gardens can be grown in small spaces, such as this rooftop patio.

Whether you choose an outdoor or indoor location to grow your edibles, you should place your plants in a spot where you will see them every day. This can either be a route you walk to enter or leave your home or in a room you use frequently. If plants are out of sight, it's easier to accidentally forget about them and miss their cues for needing water.

Once you have chosen your spot, you'll have to decide how you will obtain your plants. Many dwarf and micro varieties can be found by buying the seeds and growing them yourself under grow lights. Many of the projects in this book start with sowing seeds directly into your container of choice, but there are projects where young plants can be transplanted into the container and grouped together.

While there are always exceptions, the reality is that many of the micro food varieties available as seeds are super easy to grow. Here are some basics to get you started.

Providing enough light and water, along with a soil mix that drains well, sets your micro plants up for growing success.

## FROM HOUSEPLANTS TO EDIBLE PLANTS

If you already grow houseplants, now is the perfect time to dip your toe in the edible gardening realm by expanding your repertoire and growing your own food. You already know the ins and outs for caring for houseplants. Spoiler alert: Growing edibles is not that different!

In fact, you may already be growing houseplants that produce fruit—for example, do you grow citrus trees indoors? You will find growing micro edibles rewarding when you are able to harvest from your indoor space.

◀ To choose an indoor spot for your micro food garden, look for a level location with plenty of light. Sunny south- or west-facing windows are best.

# STARTING MICRO FOOD BY SEED

Welcome to the fun and addictive world of growing your edibles from seed!

Many of the plants that I used for projects in this book were grown from seed. When selecting what type of plants you want to grow from seed, remember that it is OK to not use all the seeds provided in your seed packet. If you are growing tomatoes, peppers, or melons from seed, you can sow a little more than you think you'll need and save the rest. If you want to grow a specific pepper plant for one project, you might only sow

You can sow seeds for melons outdoors safely after the last frost and after the ground has warmed up.

four seeds, even if the packet contains thirty. The reason why you would not just sow one seed is because you want to ensure that you have a few backups. That way you can pick the best performing one for use with your project, and you'll have extra seeds in case they do not all sprout (because despite our best efforts, we can't rely on 100% germination, no matter how fresh the seed is). If all four seeds do successfully germinate and you find yourself with extra plants by the time you are ready to plant them up, you can always share them with a friend.

On seed packets for warm weather plants, you will see recommendations for when to start growing plants from seed indoors. What type of seeds would you start this early indoors? Mainly it's tomatoes, eggplants, and peppers, but other edibles may enjoy a jump start, too. This practice ensures that plants will be large enough and further along in their growth when it is warm enough to plant them outside.

Here is how you can decode this language: Figure out when your area receives its last frost date. (For me, this is usually the last week of April.) Using this week as a guide, I count back however many number of weeks the packet tells me to. So if I was using April 28 as my first frost-free day, and a packet says *start six weeks before last frost*, I use the calendar to count back six weeks from April 28. This brings me to mid-March. So if I want my seedlings to be in good shape for the coming season, I should start the seeds in March.

For a seed packet that says I can sow directly outside after frost, I would again use this frost-free week as my guide. Examples of seeds where I would do this includes melons, cucumbers, and beans. I usually wait 2–3 weeks after the frost-free week to start warm weather seeds outside, to account for chilly nights. However, many of the micro food projects can easily be brought inside if a cold snap is forecasted.

The projects in this book will recommend how to start your plants. Many can be seeded directly in place (such as the Muffin Pan Basil). Other plants will need to be started earlier and transplanted into your container (such as the Taste of Italy project). To do this, you'll want to start your seeds in a smaller container indoors.

There are different ways to start your seeds under lights. Here are some choices to choose from:

**Plastic containers:** Seed-starting plastic cells usually feature six or eight "cells" to start your seeds. You simply fill it up with a seed-starting mix and water afterwards. These are good for plants that will need a long time to grow.

**Newspaper pots**: Newspaper pots are environmentally-friendly and can be transplanted right into your containers when the plant is ready. Choose pages that do not have color ink. These will not last as long as plastic containers, so they are good for plants that grow quickly and will not be in this container for long.

**Soil blocks**: Soil blocking is another earth-friendly way to start your seeds. It often involves making your own soil mix so the blocks stick together. This method lets you start more seeds in a smaller footprint if you start with mini soil blocks. Once those plants grow a bit larger, you will need to pop them into a larger soil block or transplant them directly into your container.

Thinning seeds is a way to ensure your plant will grow strong and reach its fullest potential. This before and after shot shows how radish seeds look before and after they are thinned.

### A NOTE ABOUT THINNING

When starting seeds, it's easy to sow a bunch of seeds in one spot, which can lead to crowding. You will need to remove them as they grow. This might seem counterintuitive—why start seeds if you plan on pulling out plants and discarding them? If you leave them all to compete for the same space, you'll get leggy, exhausted seedlings that will not grow to their full potential. It's easier not to oversow when you are planting larger seeds. It's harder to do if you are starting tiny seeds, such as carrots. Sometimes it is easier to use a scissor to go in and trim your seeds, so that way you do not disturb the roots of the plants you are saving in the process.

For projects where you want to have a lot of plants, such as lettuce, watercress, or kale for example, it is OK to be a bit heavy handed. When sowing seeds directly into your project's container, such as the Edible Side Table (page 37), you can sow extra lettuce seeds so you have enough for cut-and-come-again lettuce. The term *cut-and-come-again* refers to the practice of harvesting the young outer leaves of the plant and keeping the central growing point intact to allow for new growth to develop for future harvesting.

Some seeds, such as radishes, carrots, and beets, will likely need to be thinned after they start growing so the plants have enough space to grow as they mature.

For seeds you start indoors but will eventually move outdoors when the temperature is warmer, such as peppers, you'll need to acclimate them to life outdoors by hardening them off.

Hardening off is a term used to describe how to gradually introduce a plant that has been growing indoors to the outside world without shocking it. You'll want to gradually bring the plant outside for small bursts of time into the shade to expose it to the temperature, sun, and wind. Place it in a protected area when you are doing this. You can increase the time outside and the exposure to the sun a little more each day. Usually the plant is ready to be outside after five days of this, as long as the temperatures remain favorable.

You can set your micro edibles up for success by gradually exposing them to outdoor temps and sunlight over a series of days. This is called hardening off.

You can grow plants in many ways. Some examples include newspaper pots, plastic containers or soil blocks.

# GROWING PLANTS THAT OTHERS HAVE STARTED

Don't worry—you do not need to start all plants for your projects from seed. If your space is not yet ready to accommodate seed starting, many plants can be purchased as plant starts at your independent garden center. For some projects in this book, it is actually easier to buy the plant from the nursery than to start it from seed, such as alpine strawberries. You can grow them from seed, but it will take much longer to yield a plant that can produce strawberries.

You can still use seed catalogs to choose varieties. Make a list and reach out to your independent garden center before the growing season begins to inquire if they will be selling the micro edibles you wish to grow.

Let's take a look at four main categories that will influence how your micro gardens will take shape: containers, lighting, water, and soil choice. You will see how they all play a role in the success of your micro edible plant.

A mature alpine strawberry plant purchased at an independent garden center (left) will bear fruit much faster than a plant grown from seed (right).

# CONTAINER BASICS

There are many household items that you might already have on hand that can be repurposed as a container for micro food. Traditional growing containers also work for growing edibles and can be arranged in fun groupings. No matter which style you choose, container selection is a great way to show off your style and personality.

## FIND THE CONTAINER THAT IS RIGHT FOR YOUR MICRO FOOD

**Plastic:** This is one of the easiest containers to find at garden centers, and they come in a variety of styles and sizes, including urn planters and window boxes. You'll want to opt for a higher quality plastic for your container as opposed to cheaper ones, which could break over time. Look for planters that are marked as food-grade plastic. There are retailers who also offer plastic containers with self-watering features, which often features a water reservoir at the bottom of the container. These type of planters usually cost more, but if you plan to be traveling and leaving your plants on their own or in the care of a plant sitter, this might be a good option to try.

**Terra-cotta:** This is a popular container variety and is a good choice for plants that like to dry out a bit before being watered again. This material is made from clay and allows roots to breathe. Over time, the container might develop a white powder on the outside. No need to worry: this is actually dry salt deposits that are left behind as the water moves through the terra-cotta material through evaporation. The source for the film on the pot is either from hard water or fertilizers, but it is not harmful to your plants. Terra-cotta should not be left outdoors in cold regions because the freezing temperatures could cause the pot to crack.

**Fabric pots:** Fabric pots have grown in popularity and can be found in an assortment of sizes. You can find smaller fabric pots (1 to 5 gallons [3.8 to 19 L]) that can be used for micro veggies. The 1-gallon (3.8 L) size is the equivalent of a 6-inch (15 cm) pot. The larger, 5-gallon (19 L) size is useful for vining crops, such as melons. Fabric pots help with airflow around the roots of plants.

Micro tomatoes grow well in small terra-cotta pottery.

A miniature eggplant is at home in a glazed pot.

Hanging baskets are just one of the many options when choosing a container for your micro edibles. This variety of tomato has a cascading nature, and the hanging basket helps keep the fruit from touching the soil.

**Glazed pots:** Many decorative pottery falls in this category. You'll want to use pottery that uses a nontoxic glaze. If you are unsure of the glaze ingredients, you can always pop the plant into a smaller pot inside the larger glazed pot to achieve the desired look.

**Hanging baskets:** Hanging baskets are usually made from plastic or a wireframe with a coconut coir lining, also called a coco liner, which is lining made from the husks of ripe coconuts. Because hanging baskets are exposed to all elements, including the wind, you should check the soil regularly to make sure the plant has not dried out.

## REPURPOSED ITEMS:

**Metal:** Keep out of direct sun and do not place directly on pavement.

**Glass:** One perk of using a glass container is being able to see the roots grow. Adding drainage holes to glass jars is possible, but you'll need to drill holes at a slow speed with a special drill tip in order to prevent the glass from cracking. If your plant needs full sun, you'll need to check on it daily to make sure it does not dry out.

**Baskets:** Baskets can be used for growing edibles. You'll want to look for baskets that are not painted or dyed. Being as natural as possible is the way to go! You can use plastic to line the baskets to help keep the soil in place. Use plastic that

Seedlings can be started in disposable muffin pans. Repurposed baking items often make for great temporary containers for fast-growing edibles.

This ornamental container features design principles that can also be used when planning your edible containers. There is a "thriller, filler, and spiller" in this grouping.

is *food-safe* such as food storage bags. Food-safe means that the material is safe for contact with consumable food.

**Items found in a kitchen:** Maybe it's disposable pie plates, muffin tins, or loaf pans—these products make for great containers in small spaces.

No matter what container you choose, you'll want to make sure it offers drainage. Various projects in this book explain the best ways to add drainage holes to a variety of materials.

## WHAT SIZE CONTAINER?

The projects in this book feature small plants, which means you will not need gigantic planters to accommodate them. Many of the plants are adaptable to smaller containers, and each project includes a recommendation of the container to use. Some of the projects in this book combine a few different plants into one container, so you'll want to make sure you choose a pot large enough to accommodate all the roots. As you'll see, containers can be as small as coffee cups and as large as window boxes. Each project will come with a container recommendation, so you'll know what to buy.

When combining plants into one container, you can also keep in mind the saying, "thriller, filler, and spiller." This container garden terminology refers to how certain plants behave in a container. Good container design features one from each category: the *thriller* is the tall plant element, the *filler* is the medium size element, and the *spiller* is the plant material that hangs over the pot's edge.

# LIGHTING

Why does light matter? If you buy a shade-loving plant and leave it in full direct sun, the result could be burned leaves, intense wilting, and stress on the plant. Or, if you take a sun-loving, fruit-bearing plant and place it in a spot that only gets an hour or two of sun, the plant will stretch toward the available light and may not produce any fruit at all.

Not all edible plants want—or need—the same conditions. Use the chart below to pair your plants with the right levels of light:

Dwarf tomato seedlings can be grown indoors under grow lights until it is warm enough to move them outside.

| IF YOUR PLANT FEELS LIKE . . . | YOU WILL NEED . . . |
| --- | --- |
| A sun worshipper, thriving on the most available sunlight | Full sun: six hours or more of sunlight |
| Spending about half a day outside in the sun sounds doable | Part sun: four to six hours of sunlight |
| Being in the sun for a few hours and then welcomes the relief of the cool shade | Part shade: less than four hours of sunlight, but more than one and a half hours of sunlight (Your plant will do best in a spot that is sheltered from intense afternoon sun.) |
| Spending the whole day in shade and under the canopy of trees | Full shade: very little sunlight will reach your plant |

Paying attention to what a plant's recommended light exposure is will make for a healthier plant.

Lighting through a window can change throughout the year due to trees dropping leaves or where the sun rises and sets in the sky.

Following light requirements is one of the easiest steps you can do to grow the robust plants you are looking for.

Lucky for micro food gardeners, the plant tag or seed packet description will tell you the light preferences your plants need. Or, you can assess your space for the available light you can offer and then search for plants that will meet those needs.

Figuring out your lighting needs means jotting down notes for the space you are evaluating. For example, if you are indoors, you might notice that the light begins to stream through your kitchen window around 7:30 a.m., but then by 11 a.m., the direct light is gone. Whereas, the light in your living room is brighter from noon through 5 p.m.

Keeping track of how the sun moves throughout the seasons is especially helpful. During the cold season, I get more light in my kitchen window because the trees have dropped their leaves. But in the warmest part of the year, I actually have less light to work with in the same window because those same trees have leafed out, or produced leaves.

Grow lights offer more flexibility for growing indoors.

There's also the chance that some parts of your home will just not receive that much sunlight, no matter what time of year it is. This could be directly related to which way your home, apartment, or condo faces. Make a note of where the sun rises in the morning. (This is the east spot.) Then, make note of where it sets in the late afternoon. (This is the west spot.) Using that information, you can track where your growing space lies on the North/South/West/East grid. This can include windows, porches, side walkways, and balconies, too. A northern spot offers the most shade, while a southern spot offers more sunlight.

In general, a plant that will set fruit of any kind generally needs as much sun as possible to flourish. (Think full sun.) Leafy greens are more tolerant of part sun and part shade conditions.

One of the most challenging aspects to growing plants indoors is access to proper lighting. Of course, indoors, you can modify your area by purchasing grow lights. Grow lights come in a variety of shapes and sizes that can be used to brighten any indoor living space. (Check out the project on page 148 for information on how to build a tabletop grow light.)

If you do not have room for a grow light station, you can still grow some edibles indoors using a sunny windowsill. And then there are sprouts (page 143), which technically do not need sunlight in order to start growing!

# WATERING

Think about how you feel when you are dehydrated. Not good, right? But then if you drink too much water, you could feel bad as well. The key is the right balance of hydration to be at your best—and you want your plants to be this way, too.

Watering is one of the most important elements to container gardening. Knowing when to water is important. Finding the right balance takes practice. Containers can dry out quickly if they are set in sunny spots. You want to keep soil moist but not soaking wet all the time. In general, you do not want your micro edibles' soil to be dry for several days—especially in intense heat. Fluctuations between too little water and too much water can stress the plant, causing stunted growth, sometimes a loss of fruit, or worst case, death.

Ironically, one of the most common causes of death for indoor plants is actually overwatering. For most of your edible plants, you'll want to keep the soil moist. If you let it dry out, the plant will start to wilt. Containers of all sizes can dry out quickly, and you want to water before the plant starts to wilt.

## WHAT'S THE BEST WAY TO WATER?

Water your edibles where the plant meets the soil line. It is not necessary to water every leaf on the plant. You'll also want to provide your plant with a good soaking when you do water, as opposed to a short burst of water that just wets the surface. If your edible plant is outdoors, water in the morning before the heat of the day takes hold, so the plant has a chance to absorb the water before it evaporates.

◀ Watering your micro edibles along the soil line can prevent evaporation on hot days and help prevent plant diseases from spreading.

Because water drains repeatedly with containers, you can add a basic organic fertilizer to your watering repertoire to help replace nutrients that might have leached from the soil. (See the section on fertilizer on page 28 for more info.)

## THE IMPORTANCE OF DRAINAGE

Many of the projects in this book repurpose an object you might have in your home or pick up in a secondhand shop. Letting water escape from your new "container" is the first step.

Items such as coffee cups and cake pans will need drainage holes drilled into them, and items like bicycle baskets will need a plastic lining with holes to allow water to drain, but keep soil in place. Without drainage, your plants can sit in water, and that rots roots. You also do not want to leave standing water in plant trays or outdoors, where it can attract insects like mosquitoes.

Watering also goes hand in hand with the soil you choose to use to fill your containers. You want to choose a soil blend that allows for drainage and doesn't remain waterlogged.

# SOIL CHOICE

The soil that will be feeding your plant's roots plays an important role in the plant's overall health. If you choose a good quality blend, you'll be equipping your plants with the nutrient boost they need to grow large and luscious.

Because micro edibles are grown in containers, you will also need to resupply your plants with nutrients throughout the growing season. They will be working hard, and giving them healthy soil to grow in will help them persevere on days with weather extremes.

When choosing soil for your projects, you'll want to look for a soil mix that features either of the soil amendments perlite or vermiculite to help with air flow for your plant's roots. Luckily, that is fairly easy to do when you choose a soil blend labeled for container gardening.

You can either use the container blend soil straight from the bag or continue to customize it further before using. Some plants, such as tomatoes, melons, and peppers, will benefit from adding some compost to the soil, which will provide additional nutrients. Other plants, such as thyme, want a fast-draining blend. Adding perlite or even sand to some heavier soil blends will help water drain quickly.

When it comes to soil choices, look for a mix labeled for containers. You can also add soil amendments to your soil, such as vermiculite, perlite, and worm castings.

## WHAT'S THE DIFFERENCE BETWEEN PERLITE AND VERMICULITE?

- Perlite is volcanic glass. When heated, it expands and "pops" into white clusters that resembles Styrofoam. It is porous, meaning it has many little spaces where water and air can pass through. For this reason, when perlite is added to a soil mixture, it allows water to drain more easily and improves air flow around plant roots. Adding perlite to your soil mixture is ideal for plants that like things on the drier side.

- Think of vermiculite as a sponge. It is a mineral that is also heated until it expands, which allows it to hold up to three to four times its volume in water. It is dark to light brown in color and can shimmer in the right light (like mica). It is usually smaller in size than perlite. It helps improve air flow and water retention and is ideal for plants that like excess moisture available in the soil.

## GOING ORGANIC

Because you are growing micro edibles, you want the healthiest soil to make the most nutritious food. I like to use an organic soil blend, which means that it does not include synthetic, or chemical, fertilizers in the mix. Getting an organic certification means the company had to disclose the materials that were included in the soil blend, along with info about how the soil was packaged.

## HOW MUCH SOIL TO USE?

This can vary based on the size of your container and the size of your plant. Many of the projects in this book will refer to using "potting soil," occasionally with an additional element blended in. For most projects, an 8 dry quart bag (8.8 liters) of potting soil should do the trick! If you are creating multiple projects, you can purchase a 16 dry quart bag (17.6 liters).

## PLANTING 101

When it is time to add soil to your container, you'll want to work with a soil mix that is pre-moistened. If you pot up, or plant, your micro edible in a dried out soil blend, not only are you making the plant do more work when it is already getting used to its new surroundings, but it can be messy when you water—the water could pool up and flow over the side of your container, instead of working its way down into the roots of the plant.

If your potting soil has dried out, move it into a plastic container (a bin used to hold dishes is a good size), add some water, and stir it up. You don't want to work with super saturated soil, but adding enough water so it feels moist and fluffy will do the trick.

Now, you have your container and you have your soil. But how much should you fill in? If you are transplanting a plant, you can fill your container about ¾ full with potting soil. Make a hole for the plant so that the plant's current root ball will line up with about 1 inch (2.5 cm) below the edge of the container. Place the plant in the hole and use more soil to fill in the space around it so the entire soil line is level. You can use your hand to gently push the soil down. Next, water the plant along the soil line. Add water slowly so it has a chance to soak into the soil. I add water until it begins to drain at the bottom.

So, let's review. You want a good quality soil mixture, and you want it to be moist and ready for planting action. This criteria will help plants adapt when they are transplanted or when the seeds are sown.

But what happens after the plants have been in your container for a few weeks—or even months? This is where adding extra nutrients comes in. Water can evaporate faster in a container than in the ground—especially during heat waves—adding more stress to plants. Since you'll be watering your containers regularly, nutrients can escape with frequent watering and will need to be replenished throughout the growing season. To keep your plants well-fed throughout the season, look to organic fertilizers to safely add those nutrients back into the soil and give your plant a growing boost.

## FEED THE PLANT—AND THE SOIL

While you don't *need* to use fertilizers on your micro container plantings, I liken it to taking vitamins. You can opt not to take your vitamins and still be in good health, but you may not get all your nutrients and could have deficiencies. Or, you can take vitamins so you are getting all the nutrients you need. Adding fertilizer to your micro edible gives your plant access to nutrition that it may not get by just existing in the container.

Organic growing methods influences my choices for fertilizers, too. Synthetic (chemical) fertilizers can cause plants to grow rapidly, but they can also contain sodium, which over time is not good for your soil. With synthetic fertilizers, you are not building up the quality of the soil. When the chemical wears off, you need to blast the plant with more. Plants grow quickly because of the high nitrogen levels.

Organic fertilizers not only provide nutrients to the plant, but they often help to improve the quality of the soil, too. It builds up the microorganisms that live in the soil—and that's a great thing.

When shopping for fertilizers you can use, you'll notice three numbers separated by dashes. This represents nitrogen (N), phosphorus (P), and potassium (K). Nitrogen influences how much leafy growth a plant has. Phosphorus plays a role in root growth and flower and fruit development. Potassium is helpful for the overall health of the plant.

Organic fertilizers can be either liquid or in granular form. Read the container to find out the correct dose for your micro edible so you don't overpower your plants. (Too much fertilizer isn't a good thing, either.)

Seaweed fertilizers are easy to dilute in water.

Here are some organic fertilizers you can use on your micro edibles:

**Seaweed/Kelp:** This fertilizer is usually available in liquid form, and you will have to dilute it with water. This fertilizer works well as a "foliar drench"—which is a fancy way of saying you water the leaves. Sometimes, these fertilizers can have a "fishy" smell, but it often dissipates after a few hours.

**Worm castings:** Adding worm castings as a top-dressing is an easy way to add nutrients to the soil. It is a by-product of red wiggler worms, which are often used in worm bins. Earthworm castings can contain iron, sulfur, calcium, nitrogen, phosphorus, and potassium. It has an NPK rating of 5-5-3. Worm castings also helps water retention in the soil.

**Greensand:** This fertilizer is mined from marine sources of the clay mineral glauconite. It's bluish-green color comes from iron-potassium silicate. Greensand can be added to your soil blend before you plant. It helps plants make strong stems and roots. It can loosen clay soils and bind sandy soil. It can increase the water retention of soil.

**Rock Phosphate:** This is an all-natural mineral that is a major source of phosphorus, which benefits all types of plants. It can be added to your soil blend before you plant.

**Blood meal:** This is a source of nitrogen that promotes rapid growth and deep dark green color in leaves.

When choosing a fertilizer to use, look for organic fertilizer blends marked specifically for tomatoes or other garden vegetables. These mixtures are blended to be a bit lower in nitrogen and have higher amounts of phosphorus. Be sure to follow the directions when using these on your plantings.

Containers, lighting, watering, and soil choice . . . now that we've covered those topics, it's time to start choosing the project (or projects) that will work best in your growing space!

**GROWING TIPS**

- Adding a thin layer of rich compost on the soil line (as a top dressing) will give plants a nutrient boost.

- Before applying soil amendments or fertilizers, read the package instructions for the recommended application.

- Soil amendments, such as greensand, rock phosphate, and blood meal, can be added to your soil mixture before adding your plants.

# MICRO FOOD GROWING PROJECTS

In the following pages, you will find thirty projects that focus on growing micro edibles in a variety of ways. When deciding which project will work best for you, ask yourself what type of edibles you like to eat or make your meals with. If you love tomatoes, a project that includes that plant is a good place to start.

Project materials do not need to cost a lot of money. Many of the projects are made with materials that you can find at secondhand shops, craft stores, hardware stores, grocery stores, or online. It's a great way to tap into your creativity.

For some projects, you will need a power drill and specialized drill bits. There are also projects that feature more traditional planters, such as terracotta pots.

I created and tested all the projects in this book to make sure they would work for you. I also grew the plants in the projects—those either started by seed or acquired as young plants—to make sure they would work in the ways I describe.

Let's get started!

Bush beans can be grown in tight spaces, as shown in the Rainwater Collector with Living Wreath project (page 104).

◄ Peppers are one of the many edibles that can be grown in small spaces.

31

# LETTUCE BICYCLE BASKET

▶ THIS IS A COOL-SEASON PROJECT THAT CAN BE GROWN OUTDOORS.

In my town, I would often drive by a house that repurposed bicycles as garden ornaments. This got me thinking. Bicycle baskets are not only for pretty flowers—they can feature edibles, too.

This project repurposes a wicker bicycle basket that can be displayed on a retro bike to grow and harvest baby lettuce greens (*Lactuca sativa*). You'll want to use leaf lettuce instead of "head" lettuce for the project. Leaf lettuce will respond better to being harvested and continue to grow. You can plant them closer together and treat them as a "cut-and-come-again" mix. Another option: Add sweet alyssum (*Lobularia maritima*) to your basket. It's a beautiful edible flower that attracts beneficial insects.

The trick is to line the inside of the basket with plastic so that the wet soil will not eat away at the wicker. Lining the basket with plastic is also helpful to keep the soil within the basket so it does not escape when you water it. (Especially for baskets that don't have a supertight weave.)

## WHAT YOU'LL NEED

- A WICKER BICYCLE BASKET
- (3) 1-GALLON (3.8 L) BPA-FREE PLASTIC FOOD-GRADE STORAGE BAGS (I USED THREE TO FIT THE SIZE OF MY BASKET, BUT YOUR BASKET MAY REQUIRE MORE OR LESS.)
- SCISSORS
- SMALL STONES, SUCH AS PEA GRAVEL
- POTTING SOIL
- LETTUCE SEEDS
- OPTIONAL: DECORATIVE FABRIC RIBBON OR PLASTIC ZIP TIES IF YOUR BASKET DOES NOT COME WITH HANGING STRAPS

## THE STEPS:

**1 |** Take your plastic bags and cut the zip tops off.

**2 |** Use your scissors to cut the seam along the left and right side of each bag, stopping when you reach the bottom of the bag, so it opens as one long rectangular sheet.

**3 |** On the plastic sheet that is going to be your bottom layer, use your scissors to carefully poke holes through the plastic, evenly spaced along the layer. I made six holes in my plastic layer. This will help the water drain. Place this layer at the bottom of your basket.

**4 |** Use the remaining two pieces of plastic to line the left and right sides of the basket. You'll want these to be vertically along the interior basket wall, without overlapping and covering the bottom layer (that would prevent drainage).

**5** | Add a thin layer of small stones to help drainage. (You'll want to use small stones so they will not add a lot of weight to the basket.)

**6** | Add some potting soil. I like a mix with perlite to help the water drain, so it won't be heavy when wet and weigh down the wicker basket. Make sure the soil is premoistened before adding. Fill the soil so that there is about 1 inch (2.5 cm) remaining at the top of the basket.

**7** | After you've added your potting soil, trim off any plastic that remains above the soil line.

**8** | Sow the lettuce seeds directly into your basket or, if you have started your seeds ahead of time, you can transplant the small seedlings carefully into your basket. If you sow the seeds directly, sprinkle the lettuce seeds onto the soil. Cover lightly with more potting soil—the seed packet will include directions for how much to use.

**9** | Water your basket. I recommend using a watering can with a sprinkler head attachment.

**10** | Keep your bicycle basket planter in a protected spot until the lettuce seeds sprout. Keep the soil moist, but not soaking wet.

11 | Once your lettuce has sprouted, attach the bicycle basket to your bike's handlebars using the attached straps. If your basket did not come with straps, you can use decorative fabric ribbon or plastic zip ties to attach it. You'll want to let the lettuce seedlings grow 4 inches (10 cm) before you begin to cut and harvest baby greens for salads. You can cut the leaves using scissors. Cut at the base of the plant from the outside. See the project sidebar on page 36 for tips on harvesting your bicycle basket lettuce greens.

## TIPS FOR GROWING TANTALIZING LETTUCE

◆ ◆ ◆

Most varieties of lettuce are cool-weather crops, meaning that they grow best before the heat of the season kicks in. When growing baby greens, you'll be harvesting the lettuce before it has a chance to fully mature. Seed packets give an estimate of how long it will take for each different variety to grow, but basically, baby leaf lettuce takes half the amount of time. Generally, it's 20 days for baby leaf and 40 days for fully mature.

**PLANT VARIETIES TO TRY:** Any lettuce leaf variety will work for this project!

## HOW TO HARVEST AND KEEP GROWING

When lettuce leaves reach 4 inches (10 cm) high, cut the leaf off at the base of the plant. When you harvest your baby lettuce greens, you will want to work from the outside in. That way, the plant can continue to produce new leaves from the center. It's important not to harvest the entire plant if you want it to grow back with more leaves. (Think of it as giving it a haircut.) After a few rounds of this, your plants can be replaced with new lettuce plants, using succession sowing.

Succession sowing means that you continue to sow seeds for new plants throughout the season.

You can succession sow lettuce seeds every two weeks using different containers to have a continuous harvest. You can then transplant those baby plants into your basket as you use up your original batch. By sowing seeds every two weeks, you'll always ensure that you have more lettuce to harvest.

You can continue to grow lettuce in hot temperatures if you provide an area with shade from the heat of the sun. Or, you can take a break and begin sowing seeds when the weather gets cooler.

# EDIBLE SIDE TABLE

> THIS IS A COOL-SEASON PROJECT THAT CAN BE GROWN OUTDOORS.

## WHAT YOU'LL NEED

- RECTANGULAR WOODEN PICTURE FRAME (SEE THE PROJECT SIDEBAR FOR HOW TO CHOOSE A GOOD ONE FOR THIS PROJECT.)
- (4) METAL STRAIGHT TOP PLATE TABLE LEG BRACKETS (2½ INCH [6.5 CM])
- MARKER
- SAFETY GLASSES
- POWER DRILL
- $\frac{9}{64}$-INCH (3.6 CM) DRILL BIT
- SHEET OF COCONUT COIR (PLANT NURSERIES ARE ABLE TO CUSTOM CUT A PIECE 24 OR 36 INCHES [61 TO 91.5 CM] IN LENGTH FOR YOU.)
- CHICKEN WIRE
- WIRE CUTTERS
- WORK GLOVES
- STAPLE GUN
- FLAT BLADE SCREWDRIVER
- (4) WOODEN TABLE LEGS (1½ × 28 INCHES [4 × 71 CM])
- POTTING SOIL
- SEEDS

My grandfather was a cabinetmaker who emigrated from Germany. While he made many decorative and sophisticated pieces of furniture over the years, one of the tables I remember the most was a three-legged one he created for my mother. Instead of fashioning a fourth table leg, he was able to balance the table with only three.

When creating this living table, I thought of his three-legged creation. While I opted for the traditional four table legs, this project is a fun accent piece to use outside in a small space. Why just grow baby greens on top of a small table, when you can make a living table for micro edibles!

The greens in this table can be substituted depending on your season. You can grow lettuce, kale, or spinach seeds either exclusively or combined. You have control over the size of your table, too, by selecting the size picture frame you wish to use. (See the project sidebar on page 41 on how to choose a frame.)

If you want to make the table multipurpose—growing greens and holding beverages, for example—add a decorative tile to the center of your growing area before sowing the seeds.

## THE STEPS:

1 | Flip your picture frame upside down. Position your table leg mounting brackets in each corner of the picture frame and mark where the screws should be drilled. Put on your safety glasses. Predrill the holes in the frame using the ⁹⁄₆₄-inch drill bit, being careful not to drill completely through the picture frame. Use your drill to secure the screws in the table bracket to the frame. Drill slowly—you do not want to split the frame with too much force.

**2 |** Take the coconut coir layer and place it on top of the picture frame. Then, place the chicken wire as the next layer. Using the staple gun, begin to staple and attach the chicken wire to one long side of the picture frame, taking care not to staple near the mounting brackets.

**3 |** Extend the chicken wire across the frame and continue to roll it out so you have almost half more than the width of your frame. Carefully flip the frame over and push down on the middle of the coconut coir to create a slight depression. This is to create the "pocket" for where your edibles will grow. Bend your chicken wire where it meets the frame, so you know where to cut. Then, flip it upside down again.

**4 |** Use the staple gun to attach the bent chicken wire to the other long side of the frame, once again taking care not to staple around the mounting bracket. Wearing your work gloves, use a wire cutter to cut the chicken wire free of the roll. Using the screwdriver, fold the cut metal pieces back on itself into the coconut coir layer to avoid leaving sharp edges.

**5 |** In each corner by the mounting bracket, carefully trim the chicken wire so only a small portion remains around the bracket. Carefully fold the chicken wire into the coconut coir. Seal the sharp edges by bending them into each other.

Kale and lettuce seeds can be sown together, and both will be ready to harvest as baby greens within 20–30 days.

**6** | Secure the chicken wire on the remaining two shorter ends of the picture frame using the staple gun.

**7** | Attach the table legs. Once they are screwed in, flip the table over. Your table's coconut coir and chicken wire layer should naturally concave in the center.

**8** | Add your potting soil mixture on top of the coconut coir. Fill it so it is about level with the frame. Scatter your seeds (I used both kale and lettuce) and cover lightly with soil. Water afterwards. Your seeds should sprout within 10 days and be ready for harvesting as baby greens in 20–30 days. (Check your seed packet for the specifics on your variety.)

**VARIETIES TO GROW:** Look for any dwarf kale varieties for this project. Lettuce and spinach can both be grown as baby greens. Look for heat-resistant varieties in warmer seasons to postpone bolting. The term *bolting* refers to when a plant starts to prematurely produce flowers and go to seed in an attempt to reproduce, which can cause a poor-quality harvest and bitter leaves.

## GROWING TIP

To keep your kale looking picture-perfect, cover your lettuce table with a floating row cover when not in use. A floating row cover, also called garden fabric, is a gauze-like, white, lightweight, nonwoven fabric made from polypropylene or polyester that is used to protect plants. This will help discourage caterpillars—who also enjoy eating kale— from chewing on the leaves.

## WHAT TYPE OF PICTURE FRAME SHOULD I CHOOSE?

I recommend using a nonmetal picture frame for this project. Wooden frames work well. You can search secondhand shops or thrift stores for frames that will work well for the project or wait until your local crafts store has a sale or clearance. Look for picture frames that meet the following criteria:

- **Depth:** 1 inch (2.5 cm)
- **Size:** 8 × 10 inches (20.5 cm × 25.5 cm); 11 × 14 inches (28 cm × 35.5 cm); 20 × 24 inches (51 cm × 61 cm).

The frame needs to be thick enough to accommodate the screws that go with the table leg bracket and have corners that are wide enough for the bracket mount, too. The underside of the frame should be between 2¼ and 2½ inches (6 and 6.5 cm) to accommodate the bracket.

# HANGING GUTTER GARDEN

When floorspace is at a premium, you begin noticing ways you can effectively use vertical space. Growing vertically is often used for vining plants (such as the Melon Magic project on page 94), but it can be used for plants with a smaller root span, too.

Vertical gardens, such as this one, are ideal for keeping garden pests such as slugs away. Sometimes, the best spot for sun may not have an available footprint to grow food. Attaching this project to a wall can maximize your growing space.

## WHAT YOU'LL NEED

- SAFETY GLASSES
- WORK GLOVES
- FORGED STEEL SNIPS
- 5.5-INCH (14 CM) K-STYLE ALUMINUM GUTTER, TRIMMED TO 16 INCHES (41 CM) IN LENGTH
- 1 EACH: RIGHT AND LEFT K-STYLE GUTTER END CAPS
- POWER DRILL

- 2 DRILL BITS: ONE SMALL AND ONE LARGE (I USED AN 11/64-INCH [4.4 MM] DRILL BIT AND A 7/32-INCH [5.6 MM] DRILL BIT TO ACCOMMODATE THE DIAMETER OF MY S-HOOK.)
- WATERPROOF GLUE
- DISPOSABLE GLOVES
- MARKER
- (2) 6-INCH (15 CM) HANGING BRACKETS WITH MOUNTING HARDWARE

- SMALL STONES, SUCH AS PEA GRAVEL
- POTTING SOIL
- PERLITE (IF NEEDED TO LIGHTEN YOUR SOIL MIXTURE AND PROMOTE DRAINAGE)
- SEEDS
- (2) 6-INCH (15 CM) S-HOOKS

Growing food in rain-collecting gutters is a great way to use available wall space outdoors. But when growing food in small spaces, a long gutter (4 feet [122 cm] or longer) can be difficult to place. Here's a creative twist that uses hanging plant brackets to suspend a short, modified gutter that can be used in tight spaces. This project can work on balcony, breezeway, and garage walls.

This project is also ideal for gardeners who find difficulty in kneeling or bending over when trying to tend to their edibles. You can mount the project at a height that is easy for you to access. I chose a narrow area with the brackets mounted at eye level. You'll want to choose a spot that is protected from heavy winds.

## THE STEPS:

**1** | Wearing your safety glasses and work gloves, use the forged steel snips to cut the aluminum gutter to 16 inches (41 cm) in length. Try to make even, straight cuts.

**2** | Attach the left and right end caps to each side of the gutter. To ensure that they attach cleanly, it is helpful to line the end cap up with the gutter edge, position the gutter vertically on a table, and push down.

**3** | Still wearing your safety glasses, drill four evenly spaced drainage holes in the bottom of the gutter with the $^{11}\!/_{64}$-inch (4.4 mm) drill bit.

**4** | On each end cap, measure about ½ inch (1.5 cm) down from the top center. First, drill a hole with the $^{11}\!/_{64}$-inch (4.4 mm) drill bit. Once the hole is created, use the $^{7}\!/_{32}$-inch (5.6 mm) drill bit to drill in the same spot to enlarge the hole. This is a gradual and safe way to increase the diameter.

**5** | Wearing disposable gloves, apply a layer of waterproof glue along the inside seams of where the gutter and end caps meet. Allow the glue to dry and cure.

**6** | While your glue is drying, you can mount the hanging hardware to your wall. On the surface where you will hang the gutter, mark two spots, 16 inches (41 cm) apart. Use your power drill to attach the hanging brackets on each spot.

**7** | Next, when the glue has cured, line the bottom of the gutter with a thin layer of small stones. Fill your gutter with a lightweight potting soil. You can mix in additional perlite to aid drainage. (For 1 part potting soil, you can add ¼ part perlite.) When adding soil, make sure that the soil level is below the holes drilled on the end caps. You can either sow your seeds directly or transplant small seedlings into the gutter. I find sowing seeds directly a bit easier. Water after seed sowing or planting. Optional: If you sow seeds, you can bring your gutter indoors and place it under a grow light to "speed the growth" for germination.

**8** | Insert the S-hook into the hole on each side of the end cap. Use the S-hook to hang the gutter garden from the hanging bracket.

## SUCCESSION SOWING MADE EASY
## IN YOUR GUTTER GARDEN

Growing baby greens is a great way to yield an edible crop quickly in a small space. But not all greens can be grown throughout the year. Succession sowing is the practice of sowing a new crop in the space of one that has just finished producing.

Let's say you start off your growing season with spinach seeds in your gutter garden. Many spinach varieties will be ready for harvesting as baby greens within 20–30 days. As warmer weather slips in, the spinach plants can bolt. At this point, you can remove the spinach plants from your gutter garden and replace with a heat tolerant leafy green, such as chard.

The chard will get you through the hot days and could even last until cooler weather returns, based on how much you harvest. At this point, you have the option of removing the chard and switching back over to another type of baby greens—maybe this time you'll grow lettuce.

This pattern of growing different micro edibles in your smaller space will not only keep things interesting, but offer variety for your meals throughout your growing season.

**VARIETIES TO GROW:** Any spinach can be grown as baby leaf.

## WHAT WILL GROW IN A GUTTER GARDEN?

Gutter gardens are great for plants that have shallow roots or plants that will grow and be harvested quickly. Micro candidates include fruiting plants, like strawberries; leafy greens such as baby greens and spinach; herbs, such as mint and basil; and edible flowers, such as dwarf nasturtiums and violas.

## SPINACH TIPS

Spinach (*Spinacia oleracea*) is a cool-season green that can be grown for baby leaf harvest or when plants are fully grown. You can also sow seeds late in the warmer season so they will be ready for harvest when the weather turns cooler again. Spinach prefers moist and fertile soils. The plants can bolt when temperatures get too hot. Look for varieties that are labeled as "resistant to heat-induced bolting" if you want to try and extend your growing season.

Breeders have been working on making varieties that are more disease resistant, especially for downy mildew (*Peronospora farinosa* f. sp. *spinaciae*). When I visited the California Vegetable Trials, I learned that downy mildew is the reason bagged spinach at the store will turn into slime. It's because downy mildew is a disease that continues to develop within the bag. That's just another great reason for growing your own food!

# BABY BOK CHOY CUPS

Bok choy (*Brasssica rapa* subsp. *chinensis*), or pak choi, is a miniature Chinese cabbage that is in the brassica family. Leaf colors range from green through purple, with a lighter colored, bulbous bottom. The plant tastes similar to cabbage, and there are micro varieties available to fit the tightest of spaces. To further highlight its miniature traits, I found decorative coffee cups to use for a container. They fit well in small spaces!

For this project, you can either start the bok choy seeds directly in the coffee cup (after you drill the hole) and thin the plants as they grow. Or, you can transplant a small seedling into the cup when it has four true leaves. You'll want to provide a strong light source for the bok choy if growing indoors—either a south-facing window or under grow lights—so they do not stretch toward the light. (See the tabletop grow light project on page 148 for a setup that will work in tight spaces.)

The key to drilling ceramic is to have patience and cold water on hand. You will need to use your power drill at a slow speed throughout the project and add the cold water periodically to keep the drill bit and ceramic from overheating (which can cause your mug to crack and break).

## WHAT YOU'LL NEED

- SAFETY GLASSES
- HAND TOWEL
- CERAMIC COFFEE MUG
- TAPE (MASKING OR BLUE PAINTER'S TAPE)
- POWER DRILL
- ½-INCH (12.7 MM) DIAMOND DRILL BIT
- COLD WATER IN A SMALL WATERING CAN
- SMALL STONE
- POTTING SOIL
- BOK CHOY SEEDLING

# THE STEPS:

1 | Put on your safety glasses. Lay your towel on the table and place the coffee mug on top, upside down. Place a small piece of masking or painter's tape at the bottom where you want to drill your hole for drainage.

2 | Position your drill at a 45-degree angle and on a slow speed, begin to mark the tape on the coffee mug. You'll only want to scratch the mug at this point in order to give the drill bit something to catch as you continue to drill.

3 | Once your mug is scratched, remove the tape. Still at a 45-degree angle, continue to use the drill on a slow speed to make the mark. Add the cold water periodically as you drill, which will prevent the mug and the drill bit from overheating and cracking.

4 | As you continue to drill, move your hand so you gradually move from 45-degree angle to a 90-degree angle. Continue to add water as needed.

**5** | Once at a 90-degree angle, continue to drill at a slow speed. Do not use your weight to push into the mug (the extra force could crack it when the drill makes the final cut for the hole).

You'll know you are close to completing the hole because the drill bit sound will change—the pitch increases right before the bit makes its way through the ceramic.

**6** | Once the hole is created in the mug, turn the mug right-side up and add a small stone to cover up the hole. Add your potting soil mix.

- If you are starting seeds, scatter the seeds on top of the soil and cover lightly with soil. (Check your seed packet for the proper depth.) Water and place underneath a strong light source. As the seeds grow, you'll want to thin them so one plant remains in the mug to mature.

- If you are transplanting bok choy seedlings into the cup, use one seedling per mug. Fill the mug with more potting soil, leaving approximately ½ inch (1.5 cm) from the top. Water and either place under grow lights if growing indoors or in a sunny spot if growing outdoors.

**7** | Depending on your variety, the bok choy will be ready to harvest in 45 days.

**VARIETIES TO TRY:** Look for varieties that will stay small in size. 'Purple Lady' bok choy and 'Green Fortune' pak choi are two you can try.

## GROWING TIPS

◆ ◆ ◆

Bok choy is considered a cool season crop, so it can be planted in the spring or early fall for harvest. If you are growing it outdoors, keep an eye on the temperatures. Bok choy is a biennial plant, so if you left it to grow without harvesting, it will flower in its second year. However, in cool seasons, overnight temperatures that consistently dip below 50°F (or 10°C) might trick the plant into thinking that it's overwintering, causing it to bolt when the temperatures rise again.

Bok choy likes sun and rich, moist soil. Since this project highlights the miniature, be sure to check your coffee cup bok choy regularly to make sure the soil is not too dry. You can also grow bok choy indoors under grow lights (with air-conditioning) if the temperatures outside are too hot. It takes a bit more time to mature, but you'll end up with a beautiful plant by the time it is ready to harvest. There are lots of varieties that will grow to mini size, with either green or white stems.

Sometimes growing a new vegetable is a way to jump start your cooking routine and help you find new recipes to use. Bok choy is one of those vegetables. You can use it raw or cooked. Try adding it to salads, stir-fries, or soups. It pairs well with fish dishes or can be used in vegan dishes.

Bok choy is in the Brassica family and grows best in cool weather.

# FINGERLING POTATO WINDOW BOX

> THIS IS A BOTH A COOL- AND WARM-SEASON PROJECT THAT CAN BE GROWN OUTDOORS.

## WHAT YOU'LL NEED

- SEED POTATOES
- WINDOW BOX, WITH A LENGTH OF 24 INCHES (61 CM) OR 30 INCHES (76 CM), DEPENDING ON YOUR SPACE SIZE
- SMALL STONES, SUCH AS PEA GRAVEL
- POTTING SOIL
- COMPOST
- HANGING BRACKETS FOR THE WINDOW BOX (IF YOU CHOOSE TO MOUNT IT)

Being short on space does not mean you need to forgo growing delicious potatoes. In fact, you can grow tasty fingerling potatoes in a window box. These potatoes are small, finger-shaped, and can grow in less space than traditional potatoes, which are often grown in large hills, straw bales, or even modified garbage cans. They also come in a variety of colors and are fairly resistant to disease. Fingerling potatoes are fully mature and ready to be eaten as soon as they are harvested.

This project calls for seed potatoes, which are potatoes that are not treated with a sprout inhibitor. Sprout inhibitors can be applied to potatoes

available in grocery stores in an attempt to extend the shelf life. Let your seed potatoes be exposed to moderate lighting for about a week before you plan to plant.

The window box will need a little maintenance as the plants grow because you will need to add more soil. Deeper window boxes are ideal for this, but you can grow fingerling potatoes in standard size window boxes, too. (You may get a few less potatoes as a result.) Continuing to add soil as the potatoes grow will pay off with tasty spuds at the end of the season. (For window box options, check out the sidebar on page 84.)

## THE STEPS:

1 | You will not need many seed potatoes to get started. On the first day, you will cut your seed potatoes into 1½- to 2-inch (4 cm to 5 cm) pieces that contain an "eye," or sprout. Once the potatoes are cut, leave them on a plate for the edges to dry out, or cure. They should be ready for planting on the second day.

2 | After your potatoes have cured, take your window box and fill it with a layer of small stones. Fill the window box with a layer of your potting soil mix (no more than a 1 inch [2.5 cm] high). Next, add a scoopful of compost to the window box and blend the two soils together.

**3** | Add your potato pieces, with the cut side facing down and the eyes facing up, spacing them approximately 3 inches (7.5 cm) apart.

*Note:* This is closer than you would plant the potatoes if you were growing them in a raised bed or directly in the ground. Cover with a thin layer of soil. Water lightly.

**4** | Place your window box with the potatoes in a sunny spot. As the potatoes begin to grow, you can gradually add more soil to the box to continue to cover up the stem. Do this until you fill the window box and have about a ½-inch (1.5 cm) gap remaining. The new potatoes will grow in this soil.

**VARIETIES TO TRY:** Look for fingerling potatoes described as being small to medium in height. Some fingerling potatoes will produce taller plants. Also consider whether you want to grow early-, mid- or late-season varieties.

As the season progresses, the potatoes will grow about 15–18 inches high (38–46 cm). Some varieties are a bit taller, so be sure to read the description. If you decide to not mount the window box, you can set them up on a rock wall or along a walkway. I grew mine in my front walkway next to my mailbox.

If you can find blue or purple potatoes, even better. They will give you a dose of anthocyanins, a naturally occurring antioxidant. Who knew that being healthy would be so delicious, too?

Fingerling potatoes are ready for meal prep shortly after harvesting.

# TIPS FOR GROWING DELICIOUS SPUDS

Potatoes (*Solanum tuberosum*) thrive in well-drained but moisture-retaining soil. Potatoes are heavy feeders, so add good-quality organic compost in your container. You can plant potatoes outside when the threat of frost has passed. The new potatoes will grow in the soil as you cover up the stems. By adding more soil to the window box, you are preventing sunlight from reaching your new potatoes, which could turn the potatoes green. (Do not eat potatoes that are green—they can be toxic.)

Flea beetles can be a nuisance and will leave tiny pinholes in your potato's leaves. You can sprinkle a thin layer of diatomaceous earth on leaves very early in the morning to try and mitigate the damage. Keep an eye out for potato beetles, too. They can defoliate the plant rather quickly. Hand pick the beetles off the plants and place into a cup of soapy water. Floating row covers used early in the season can help mitigate the damage of both.

Once the potatoes begin to flower, you will know the harvest time is near. Keep the plants well-watered. Fingerling potatoes can be harvested at this stage, or you can wait a bit longer until the plants die back after flowering. Potatoes can be left in the ground for up to two weeks after the foliage has died back.

Because fingerling potatoes have a thin skin, you'll need to be careful when harvesting them. Tip your window box on its side onto newspaper and ease the plants out of their container. Use your hands to gently pull apart the plants and shake the potatoes free. Brush off the soil, but do not rinse them off with water until you are ready to use them in the kitchen.

Fingerling potatoes do not store as long as regular potatoes, so break out that recipe book and whip up something delicious.

# EDIBLE FLOWERS

▶ THIS IS BOTH A COOL- AND WARM-SEASON PROJECT THAT CAN BE GROWN OUTDOORS.

I have a soft spot for flowers. They offer so many great qualities, especially in edible gardens. Their bright petals help attract pollinators, they can punctuate green sceneries with a pop of color—and best yet—there is a whole category of flowers that are edible, too.

When I worked as a pastry chef, I would love to decorate cakes with edible flowers. The sugar-inspired flowers look lovely in their own right, but there is something about a cake decorated with pansies and violas, or a cupcake garnished with petals, that really catches my eye.

This project was inspired by the coffee cans at the grocery store. No—really! I was eyeing them and thinking how they would be a good size for planters. But they needed to be jazzed up a bit—plain wouldn't do. That's where the idea to spray paint them with chalkboard paint came in, and instantly, a rainy day project that involved decorating and planting the containers came to mind.

## WHAT YOU'LL NEED

- AN EMPTY METAL COFFEE CAN (A 26-OUNCE [765 ML] CAN WORKS WELL, BUT SMALLER SIZE COFFEE CANS ARE ALSO EFFECTIVE.)
- CHALKBOARD SPRAY PAINT
- MASK
- SAFETY GLASSES
- DISPOSABLE GLOVES
- CHALK
- POWER DRILL
- ¹¹⁄₆₄-INCH (4.4 MM) DRILL BIT
- COFFEE FILTER
- POTTING SOIL
- FLOWER SEEDS (FOR SUGGESTIONS, SEE THE CHART ON PAGE 59.)
- OPTIONAL ITEMS: RAFFIA RIBBON, SISAL ROPE, OR JUTE BRAIDED RIBBON TO TIE AROUND THE COFFEE CAN; CHALKBOARD MARKERS, FOR DECORATIONS

The best way to ensure that your flowers are organic and pesticide-free is to grow your own from seed. Some independent garden centers that follow organic practices and purchase from reputable plant suppliers will also be able to offer organic young plants.

There are many varieties of edible flowers that can be used for this project. (See the chart opposite.) You can use the planted coffee cans as an outdoor table centerpiece or as a hostess gift for summer parties. You can plant them up with mature plants a few days before the event.

## THE STEPS:

**1** | The day before you want to plant your seeds, use the chalkboard spray paint to cover the can. Wearing your safety glasses, a mask, and disposable gloves, aim to apply even coats, stopping in between to turn the can to cover all sides. Follow the directions on the spray paint container for best coverage. Allow for the paint to dry 24 hours.

**2** | The next day when the paint has dried, prep the chalkboard surface with chalk (as directed on the paint can). Wash off the chalk with water.

**3** | Again wearing your safety glasses, drill three to four drainage holes into the bottom of your coffee can. Turn right-side up and add a coffee filter to the bottom of the can. Fill with potting soil—either ¾ way full if planting seeds or half way if transplanting a small flower. Water after planting.

**4** | Use chalk or chalkboard markers to decorate the container. If you are gifting this project, perhaps your illustration will include info on the edible flower growing inside. Create custom name tags that you can attach by punching a hole and threading through with raffia ribbon, sisal rope, or jute braided ribbon.

**5** | Continue to monitor your container and water as needed as your seeds begin to grow. Follow directions on your seed packet for the best lighting conditions.

## GARNISH YOUR PLATES WITH THE FOLLOWING MICRO PRETTY PETALS

• • •

There are many edible flowers, but here are some varieties that stay petite in size, making them easy to pair up with your other micro edibles.

| FLOWER | TASTE | TYPE | PRO TIP |
|---|---|---|---|
| NASTURTIUMS (*Tropaeolum minus*) | Peppery | Choose a mounding variety that will not grow larger than 12 inches (30.5 cm). | Soak seeds in water for 12 to 24 hours before planting in the container. |
| CALENDULA (*Calendula officinalis*) | Peppery | Look for varieties that grow between 10 and 12 inches (25.5–30.5 cm). | Fresh or dry petals can be substituted for saffron in recipes. |
| PANSIES AND VIOLAS (*Viola cornuta*) | Similar to lettuce | Choose a mounding variety. | You do not need to remove the petals—they can be eaten whole. Can be crystalized with sugar and used for desserts. |
| VEGETABLE PEA FLOWERS (*Pisum sativum*)∗ | Just like peas! | Choose a dwarf variety. | Soak seeds in water for 12 to 24 hours before planting. |
| STRAWBERRY (*Fragaria vesca*) | Mild strawberry flavor | Look for runner-less alpine strawberry plants. | Petals can be used in salads. |
| SWEET ALYSSUM (*Lobularia maritima*) | Similar to kale | Any variety. | Petals can be added to salads or omelets. |
| CHIVES (*Allium schoenoprasum*) | Mild onion flavor | Any variety. | Break apart blossoms before sprinkling on salads. |
| DILL (*Anethum graveolens*) | Milder flavor than the seed | Look for dwarf, fernleaf varieties. | Flowers can be added to fish dishes or omelets. |
| FRENCH MARIGOLD (*Tagetes patula*) | Citrus taste | Look for plants that grow a maximum of 12 inches (30.5 cm) high. | Eat in moderation, but can be added to salads and seafood dishes. |
| OREGANO (*Origanum vulgare*) | Zesty and strong | Snip flowers from plants that have bolted. | Blossoms can be added to bread recipes or used in Italian food dishes. |

∗ Only vegetable pea flowers are edible. Do not eat sweet pea flowers (*Lathyrus odoratus*), which look similar but are toxic.

Nasturtiums offer edible petals and leaves—try adding them to your salads for a peppery taste. The seeds are also large, making planting the seeds easier for even the smallest of gardeners.

## SOME THINGS TO REMEMBER

• Do not eat flowers that come from florists, plants at grocery stores, or big box stores.

• If you have hay fever, asthma, or allergies, do not eat flowers.

• Before using your edible flowers, dip them in a bowl of water to clean and shake free any insects that might be hiding between the petals.

Edible flowers can make everyday meals, desserts, and beverages a special occasion.

## WAYS TO USE YOUR EDIBLE FLOWERS

- **Decorative ice cubes:** Take your ice cube tray and fill with a thin layer of water and place it in the freezer. When the water is frozen, take the tray back out and place your flower petals or small flowers (face down) into the ice cube tray. Fill the tray with water and return to the freezer. Break them out to make lemonade and iced tea a special treat. The best flowers to use are small violas (the entire blossom is safe) and calendula petals.

- **Salad décor—and subtle flavors:** Use the colorful petals to add color to your greens. The best flowers to use are chives and nasturtiums.

- **Cake garnishes:** Flowers can be candied and added as cake decorations. The best flowers to use are violas, pansies, and strawberry flowers.

- **Water infusers:** Pair edible flowers with cucumber slices or lemon wedges to add subtle flavor to your water. The best flowers to use are vegetable pea flowers and strawberry flowers.

## TIPS FOR GROWING EDIBLE FLOWERS FROM SEED

To have complete control over the petals you put on your plate, you can grow edible flowers from seed.

- Nasturtium, calendula, vegetable peas, alyssum, and chives can all be direct sown into your container and placed in a warm, sunny spot.

- Pansies and violas can also be sown directly into the container but need to be covered with newspaper and placed in a cool spot to germinate. Once the seeds sprout, you can move them into the sun.

- Alpine strawberries can also be started from seed, but they will take a long time to grow. For a quicker harvest, purchase organic plants from a trusted plant nursery.

# MINI STIR-FRY GARDEN

Wouldn't it be great to have a wall of hanging ingredients that you can choose from when making your meals? The Stir-Fry Garden was based on this idea and is ideal if you have a bright and sunny spot to set it up.

There are many "ingredients" you can grow for your hanging Stir-Fry Garden. I chose to grow baby swiss chard, scallions, and tat soi, an Asian green. You can also grow mustard plants as baby greens, mini pea plants, and spinach greens.

To make the best use of space, I used three tin containers and used macramé cord to create a tiered hanging planter. I made my Stir-Fry Garden three tiers so I could grow three different types of micro edibles, but if your space only allows for one or two containers, you can modify this project as needed.

To minimize the weight of the hanging planter, I used screen mesh on the bottom of the container to help with drainage. To water, bring your hanging garden to the sink so the excess water can drain.

## WHAT YOU'LL NEED

- 3 TIN RECTANGULAR CONTAINERS (THEY CAN BE ALL THE SAME SIZE OR ONE SLIGHTLY LARGER ONE FOR THE BOTTOM LAYER. LOOK FOR A CONTAINER THAT IS 10 INCHES [25.5 CM] LONG.)
- SAFETY GLASSES
- POWER DRILL
- 11/64-INCH (4.4 MM) DRILL BIT
- NAIL FILE
- INSECT SCREEN MESH (NOT METAL)

- SCISSORS
- 70 MM (2¾-INCH) WOODEN RING
- (2) 5 MM (³⁄₁₆-INCH) MACRAMÉ CORDS, MEASURED OUT TO 12 FEET (3.7 METERS) EACH IN LENGTH
- HANGING BRACKET KIT OR OVER-THE-DOOR HANGER
- POTTING SOIL
- SEEDS OR YOUNG SEEDLINGS
- PLASTIC WRAP (IF SOWING SEEDS)

## THE STEPS:

**1** | Turn your rectangular container so the shorter side is facing you. Drill two holes on each side for the macramé cord to be threaded through. Measure 1 inch (2.5 cm) from the top. Put on your safety glasses and using your power drill, drill two holes into the side of the container. Repeat on the opposite side. Use a nail file to smooth out any rough edges on the inside of the container from the drilled holes. Repeat for all containers.

**2** | If your container does not have drainage holes, you can add four to the bottom of the container in a diamond shape. Take the insect screen mesh and cut out a piece that will fit inside the bottom of the container. Set aside.

**3** | Take your wooden ring and macramé cord and use a Lark's Head Knot to secure both cords to the ring: Fold each cord in half and place the loop over the wooden ring (A).

Then, pull each cord through the loop to tighten. This will attach the cord to the ring. Once attached to the ring, each cord will measure 6 feet (1.8 m) in length (B).

**4** | Next, you will make five spiral stitches with your cords. Spread out your cords from left to right, with the cord furthest to the left being cord 1, followed by cord 2, cord 3, and ending with cord 4 being the furthest to the right. Begin by taking cord 1 and bend it so it is on top of cords 2 and 3, but underneath cord 4.

**5** | You will then take cord 4 and bend it so it is underneath cords 2 and 3, but on top of cord 1 (A). Pull both cords 1 and 4 so they tighten around cords 2 and 3 (B).

**6** | Repeat steps 4 and 5 two more times.

**7** | Reverse direction for the cords. Beginning with cord 4, bend it so it is on top of cords 2 and 3, but underneath cord 1.

**8** | Take cord 1 and bend it so it is underneath cords 2 and 3, but on top of cord 4. Pull both cords 1 and 4 so they tighten around cords 2 and 3.

## GROWING MINI PEAS

♦ ♦ ♦

I find peas (*Pisum sativum*) one of the easiest vegetables to grow! They are able to be planted outside early in the growing season and will sprout in soil that is 45°F (7.2°C). You can purchase a soil thermometer if you are eagerly awaiting the time to plant outside. Pea plants can also be started in containers and grown indoors in a sunny windowsill. Soak seeds in lukewarm water for 12–24 hours before planting to speed up germination.

When looking for micro size pea plants to grow, explore the snap and shelling pea categories of garden catalogs. This cool-weather plant prefers full sun and fertile and moist soil. When planting in a container, use a potting soil mixture with perlite and add earthworm casings to the mix for an additional nutrient boost.

And remember—the more you harvest, the more they will grow!

**9** | Repeat steps 7 and 8 two more times.

**10** | Repeat steps 4 and 5 two more times. You will now have a simple spiral design.

**11** | You will now make two overhand knots to tie the four cords into two main cords. Fan out your cords so cord 1 is furthest to the left, and cord 4 is furthest to the right. Using cords 1 and 2, measure 4 inches (10 cm) down from your spiral stitch. Fold the cord into a loop and then pull the cords through the loop. Tighten the cord to make the knot.

Do the same for cords 3 and 4: measure 4 inches (10 cm) down from your spiral stitch, fold the cord into a loop, and then pull the cords through the loop. You'll want both knots to be horizontally even, and you can move the knot for alignment before you tighten your cord. You'll be left with two sets of cords: one on the left and one on the right.

**12** | Now, you will attach the first container. Beginning with the left side, take cord 1 and thread it through the drilled hole furthest away from you. Pull it through so it is about 8 inches (20.5 cm) down from your overhead knot. Thread the cord into the adjacent drilled hole and pull it back out.

You will repeat this step with the right side and the other two cords. Make sure your cords are aligned and the planter is horizontally balanced.

**13** | Beginning with the left side of the planter, make a knot on each cord that has been pulled through the second hole. The knot will be on the outside of the container. Pull the cord to where it entered the first drilled hole and tie a double knot on the outside of the container.

Take your second cord and tie to the first knot (where the cord came out of the container). This will distribute the weight of the planter.

Repeat step 13 for the right side of the planter.

**14** | You will attach a second planter underneath the first. On the cord, measure 10 inches (25.5 cm) down from the first container and then proceed with threading the cords to each side of the container. This time, when threading the cords, you will notice that on both the left and right side, there is one longer cord. Use the longer cord to thread through the drilled hole closest to you on the second container. (This is the opposite of how you threaded the first container.) Thread it through to the opposite hole, pull it through, and tie a knot on the outside of the container. Bring the cord back to where it was threaded through the first drilled hole and tie a double knot on the outside of the container. Take your second cord and tie to the first knot (where the cord came out of the container). This will distribute the weight of the second planter. To make sure the two containers are hanging properly, hold your project up by the wooden ring and check the knots. If anything is out of place, adjust it now.

**15** | Add the last container to your project. Measure 10 inches (25.5 cm) down on your cord. Using the longer of the two cords and threading it through the drilled hole closest to you, repeat step 14 to attach your last container. When attaching the second cord and tying it to the first knot, make a double knot.

**16** | Check that all three containers are hanging properly by holding your project up by the wooden ring and check the knots. Adjust if needed. Take the cords and finish with an overhand knot (the knot you made in step 11). Trim off the excess cord.

**17** | Hang up your container, using either a hanging bracket or an over-the-door hook. Place the insect mesh layer in the bottom of each container.

**18** | Fill your containers with potting soil, plant your seeds or young seedlings, and then water.

- If you are transplanting young seedlings into your containers, fill the potting soil about halfway. Add your micro plants and fill the gaps with more potting soil. Water your plants.

- If you are planting seeds, fill ¾ of the container with potting soil. Follow the directions on your seed packet for sowing and then top with the recommended amount of potting soil. Water your seeds and then cover the tops with a layer of plastic wrap. When seedlings emerge, you can remove this.

## USING TAT SOI IN STIR-FRIES

♦ ♦ ♦

Tat soi (*Brassica rapa*) is an Asian green that is a great final addition to stir-fry dishes, giving a mild mustard flavor to your dish. There are several stir-fry recipes that use this edible, and growing your own to have on hand is easy. The plant is fast-growing and creates spoon-shaped leaves. The crunchy stems can be used like you would use celery, and the leaves can be used in the same way you would use spinach. You can harvest the leaves like other baby green varieties. It is related to bok choy, but has a stronger flavor. It takes about 21 days to reach the baby leaf stage and 45 days to reach full size.

**WANT MORE VARIETY FOR YOUR STIR-FRY MEAL?** Try growing your own sprouts (see page 143) and pea shoots (see page 160).

# BASKET ROOT GARDEN

> THIS IS A COOL-SEASON PROJECT THAT CAN BE GROWN EITHER INDOORS OR OUTDOORS.

Root crops such as radishes (*Raphanus sativus*) and beets (*Beta vulgaris*) can be multipurpose—not only do you harvest their roots, but you can use their greens, too. With both, you plant tiny seeds, and weeks later, you'll be unearthing root crops in its place. I wanted to incorporate the satisfaction of growing root plants but without the large fabric pots or raised beds.

When looking for a basket to use, look for an item that is approximately 5 to 6 inches high (13 to 15 cm). This will provide the minimum depth to grow your micro crop. I used a metal basket with handles to provide stability and make moving a snap. Inside the basket, I sowed miniature varieties of radishes and beets. The basket was small enough to fit on a sunny countertop, an outside table, or under a grow light.

When sowing your seeds, try not to oversow; otherwise, you will need to thin them later. They may be small and mighty, but they need their space, too.

## WHAT YOU'LL NEED

- SMALL BASKET: MINIMUM OF 5 INCHES (13 CM) HIGH AND 12 INCHES (30.5 CM) WIDE (I USED A METAL BASKET.)
- COCONUT COIR LINER (I USED A 14-INCH-(35.5 CM)- DIAMETER LINER, BUT THIS WILL CHANGE DEPENDING ON THE SIZE OF YOUR BASKET.)
- SCISSORS
- POTTING SOIL
- MINIATURE RADISH, CARROT, OR BEET SEEDS

## THE STEPS:

1 | Take your metal basket and place the coconut coir liner inside. Trim off the excess with scissors so the liner is level with the basket's edge.

2 | Fill the basket and liner with your potting soil.

3 | Sow the seeds. Aim to scatter a few about, but try not to be heavy handed. (You can always thin your plants later as they grow.)

4 | Cover with the recommended soil as directed on the seed packet and water. Place in a warm, sunny spot as you wait for the seeds to emerge.

### THIN SEEDLINGS FOR BETTER YIELDS

• • •

At first, sowing many seeds and then removing ones that are too close might seem odd. Why remove plants when you want to grow them for harvest? But in order for your root crops to reach the size they need, they need space around to grow. For example, three or four radish seedlings clustered together will never form full-size radishes.

When the plants have formed their first true leaves, you can start to remove seedlings that are too close together, leaving one in its spot. Check your seed packet for recommended spacing, or thinning, but in general, you will want to give your root crops ¾ to 2 inches (2 to 5 cm) of space between plants. You can use scissors to snip the extra plants out in order to not disturb the roots of the plants you plan to keep.

**PLANT VARIETIES TO TRY:** Look for varieties that are marked as mini and form "baby" roots. Plant descriptions that include the ability to grow in shallow soil is also a good trait.

# STRAWBERRY CAKE STAND

> **THIS IS A WARM-SEASON PROJECT THAT CAN BE GROWN OUTDOORS.**

## WHAT YOU'LL NEED

- SAFETY GLASSES
- 3-PIECE ALUMINUM CAKE PAN SET (I USED AN 8-INCH, 6-INCH, AND 4-INCH [20.5 CM, 15 CM, AND 10 CM], WITH A HEIGHT OF 2 INCHES [5 CM]. THE DEEPER THE CAKE PAN, THE MORE ROOM FOR YOUR PLANT'S ROOTS TO GROW.)
- TOWEL
- C-CLAMP
- MARKER
- POWER DRILL
- DRILL BITS, RANGING IN SIZE FROM ¹¹⁄₆₄-INCH (4.4 MM) TO ½-INCH (12.7 MM)
- (11) ½- × 13-INCH (1.5 × 33 CM) HEX NUTS: 5 FOR THE BASE AND 6 FOR SECURING THE CAKE PANS
- (11) ½-INCH (1.5 CM) GALVANIZED FLAT WASHERS: 5 FOR THE BASE AND 6 FOR SECURING THE CAKE PANS
- WATERPROOF CLEAR GLUE
- DISPOSABLE GLOVES
- 18-INCH (46 CM) STEEL THREADED ROD, ½ INCH DIAMETER (1.5 CM)
- POTTING SOIL
- ADJUSTABLE WRENCH
- 6 ALPINE STRAWBERRY PLANTS (NO LARGER THAN A 4-INCH [10 CM] POT PER PLANT IF POTTED, OR YOU CAN USE BARE ROOT PLANTS)
- OPTIONAL: 6 PACK OF SWEET ALYSSUM PLANTS, OR SMALL SEEDLINGS IF GROWING YOUR OWN

This project blends the whimsy of the cake-decorating world with gardening. By using cake pans and repurposing them as containers for alpine strawberry plants, you can create a fun centerpiece for a table—indoors or outdoors. For contrasting leaf shapes, you can tuck in sweet alyssum plants in between the strawberries.

What makes the project come together is the hardware. I opted to use a steel threaded rod to provide stability and help secure the two top cake pans to the proper height. The key to drilling the cake pans is to start with a smaller size drill bit and gradually increase to the largest drill bit. Enlarging the diameter of the hole slowly will give you better results.

After your cake stand is assembled, the easiest way to add the alpine strawberries is by using younger plants that won't mind being trans-planted into the cake pans. When buying your plants, do a spot check: gently pop them out of the container and check that your strawberries are not rootbound. At the end of the growing season, the strawberry plants can be transferred to a larger container to overwinter.

## THE STEPS:

**1** | With your safety glasses on, take your larg-est of the three cake pans and place it upside down on top of a towel on your work table. Use a C-clamp to hold the cake pan in place. Mark the center of the pan where you want to drill the hole for the rod. Start with an $^{11}/_{64}$-inch (4.4 mm) drill bit to drill the center hole, using a slow setting. Use this size drill bit to also add two drainage holes on either side of your center hole.

**2** | Use a drill bit two sizes up from where you started and redrill the center hole in the cake pan. Repeat this until you have drilled the center hole with the ½-inch (12.7 mm) drill bit. To remove sharp edges, take the ½-inch (12.7 mm) drill bit and run it through the hole to knock out any sharp edges.

**3** | Repeat steps 1 and 2 for the two additional cake pans. Set aside when finished.

**4** | On the bottom of the largest cake pan, take 5 hex nuts and 5 washers and wearing disposable gloves, glue them to the cake pan in a pentagonal pattern. Glue the washer to the pan first and then the hex nut. Allow the glue to set for the recommended time on the bottle.

**5** | Once the glue has set, turn the cake pan over. At what will be the bottom of your cake stand, thread a nut and then a washer on to the metal rod about ½ inch (1.5 cm) up. Next, add your largest cake pan (open end facing up) and then an additional washer and nut below the cake pan. This will serve as the base of your cake stand.

**6** | Starting from the top of the rod, thread a nut down about halfway. (I used my strawberry plant to measure where I wanted the next cake pan to sit, so the plant would not be crushed.) Add a washer and then the medium size cake pan. Add an additional washer and nut to secure the cake plan in place.

**7** | At the top of the rod, thread a nut down about a ½ inch (1.5 cm) from the top. Add a washer and then your smallest cake pan. Add a washer and nut to secure this cake pan to the rod.

**8** | Now, you can start planting! Add a thin layer of your potting soil mix to each layer. I planted three strawberries on the bottom layer in a triangle shape. I then added two alyssum plants in between the strawberry plants. I filled in the rest of the cake pan with soil.

9 | For the middle layer, add two strawberry plants so they face away from each other. Plant two alyssum plants in between. Fill in the rest of the cake pan with soil.

10 | For the top layer, plant one alpine strawberry plant.

11 | Water your cake pans and allow your plants to acclimate to their new home. The next day, you can move the cake stand into full sun. Be sure to check the plants when the soil is dry and add more water as needed. I find it easiest to water with the mister setting on my hose.

### GROWING ALPINE STRAWBERRIES FROM SEED

You can grow alpine strawberries from seed—they might even fruit in the first year—if you start them indoors under grow lights in late winter. The seeds need light to germinate, which may take several weeks, but once sprouted, the plants can grow quickly. I've had success growing them from seed and potting them up into larger pots as they grow. The smaller plants are easy to transplant into your Strawberry Cake Stand, too.

### WHY ALPINE STRAWBERRIES AND NOT REGULAR STRAWBERRY PLANTS?

The main reason to choose alpine strawberries (*Fragaria vesca*) for micro food projects is because they will stay compact in size. They will not send out runners like the larger berried, commercially produced strawberry (*Fragaria × ananassa*), which can quickly take over lots of space in a short period of time. The alpine strawberry plant will flower and set fruit throughout the growing season. The fruits are smaller than traditional strawberries (only about 1 inch [2.5 cm] long), but packs a strong flavor.

# MICRO FOOD FOUNTAIN

> THIS IS A WARM-SEASON PROJECT THAT CAN BE GROWN OUTDOORS.

## WHAT YOU'LL NEED

- 14-INCH (35.5 CM) TERRA-COTTA POT
- 9-INCH (23 CM) TERRA-COTTA POT
- 5-INCH (13 CM) TERRA-COTTA POT
- OPTIONAL: 3-INCH (7.5 CM) TERRA-COTTA POT
- 14-INCH (35.5 CM) TERRA-COTTA SAUCER
- SMALL STONES, SUCH AS PEA GRAVEL
- POTTING SOIL
- SEEDS AND/OR PLANTS

Micro edibles will reach new heights when they are planted in this stacked terra-cotta "fountain." While it may not provide moving water like a traditional fountain, it does add dramatic effect to your front entryway or balcony. It also takes advantage of a small footprint, being fully customizable depending on your available space and how tall you want it to be. The best part—it allows you to grow a little bit of everything.

When I built my fountain, I decided to use a 14-inch (35.5 cm) terra-cotta pot for the base layer. If your space is narrow, you can start with a 10-inch (25.5 cm) pot. In my bottom layer, I grew pink and red-stemmed chard. As you build the fountain, you bury a little bit of the pot into the previous layer you worked on. To add more color as the fountain ascended, I planted dwarf marigolds and bush beans in the next layer, followed by a Shishito pepper, which added additional height and glossy green peppers. To draw attention away from the stem of the pepper, I added a fourth planter, which happened to also be fashioned as a head planter, with thyme "hair." (For more ideas for head planters, see page 122.)

You could also have a theme with this project, such as the "tomato only" terra-cotta fountain. Each layer can feature a micro or hanging basket tomato, paired with miniature basil plants and nasturtiums. For more container planting combinations, see the project sidebar on page 77.

## THE STEPS:

**1** | This project is best assembled in its permanent spot, so you do not have to move it after it is built. Place the largest pot on top of the terra-cotta saucer. Add a layer of small stones for drainage, followed by potting soil. You will fill the pot about halfway with soil.

**2** | Place your medium size pot into the larger terra-cotta planter, slightly off center with more free space in the front.

Once the second pot is level, I fill in more soil in the base pot. If I am adding small plant starts, I will plant them now in the largest pot and fill in the soil so about 1 inch (2.5 cm) remains from the top of the pot line. If I am sowing seeds, I fill in the soil so it is level (also about 1 inch [2.5 cm] remaining from the top) and then sow the seeds.

**3** | Add a layer of small stones to the medium pot and then fill in the soil about halfway. You will then take your smallest pot and place it inside the medium pot. It will be slightly off center with more room toward the front. Make sure the smallest pot is nestled into the medium pot and then add soil around the smaller pot, filling in the medium pot. I follow the same step for planting or sowing seeds as in step 2.

**4** | Add a thin layer of small stones and then potting soil to the smallest pot. You can plant directly into this pot or bring the soil about 1 inch (2.5 cm) from the top pot lip and sow your seeds.

**5** | Bonus round! If you have an even smaller pot, you can add this to the top layer in a similar fashion. This one does not need to be as deeply buried as the first three—a slight depression in the soil is enough to hold this one in place. You can add your plant or seeds to this layer (which will likely house only one plant due to its smaller size).

**6** | With all your plants and or seeds in place, carefully water all layers of the fountain. The water from the top layer will drain through to the bottom, but I make a point to water each layer to settle the plants and seeds.

## SUGGESTED COMBOS FOR YOUR STACKED FOUNTAIN

◆ ◆ ◆

There are so many ways to customize! Here are some plant combos that work well.

### FOR A POP OF COLOR:

Shishito pepper (*Capsicum annuum*), chard (*Beta vulgaris*), and bush beans (*Phaseolus vulgaris*)

### FOR COMPANION PLANTING:

Cutting celery (*Apium graveolens*), dwarf carrots (*Daucus carota* var. *sativus*), and micro tomatoes (*Solanum lycopersicum*)

### TOTALLY TOMATOES:

A hanging basket variety of micro tomatoes (*Solanum lycopersicum*) and Greek basil (*Ocimum minimum*)

### SALAD BLEND:

Baby lettuce greens (*Lactuca sativa*), bunching dill (*Anethum graveolens*), and arugula (*Eruca sativa*)

### BERRIES, FLOWERS, AND GREENS:

Alpine strawberry (*Fragaria vesca*), dwarf French marigolds (*Tagetes patula*), and spinach (*Spinacia oleracea*)

### COOL COMBO:

Baby cabbage (*Brassica oleracea*), dwarf peas (*Pisum sativum*), and nasturtium (*Tropaeolum minus*)

Peppers (*Capsicum annuum*) benefit from full sun and well-draining soil. There are many varieties to choose from that are bred for containers, including jalapeño, bell, Shishito, and cayenne. (See the different types of peppers you can grow for spices on page 90.)

Peppers, on average, will need to be started indoors 6–8 weeks before your last average frost date. I grow mine under grow lights and use a heating mat to improve germination speed. (However, you can grow them from seed without a heating mat—they will just take a little longer to germinate.) Like tomatoes, peppers will benefit from being potted up as they grow indoors under lights until you are ready to plant them in their permanent location. If flowers form early while they are still indoors, I pinch them off so the plant can focus on growing a bit larger.

Peppers will need to be hardened off before they are set outside. If you are growing tomatoes, both peppers and tomatoes can be hardened off at the same time and in the same way. They are both warm season plants and do best when night temperatures remain in the 50°F (10°C) range. (See page 85 on growing and hardening off tomatoes.)

Choose a container for your pepper that allows it enough space for the roots to grow. While large full-sized pepper varieties will gladly grow in large containers, dwarf and container varieties do well in smaller size pots. In the stacked food fountain, I planted the Shishito pepper in the top pot—the 5-inch (13 cm) size.

Peppers range from mild and sweet to those that are hot and make you weep. Look for varieties that will stay under 24 inches (61 cm) tall.

When harvesting peppers, use pruners to cut the stem above the pepper, leaving a little stem with the plant. Do not twist the peppers off the plant.

One pest to keep an eye out for are aphids. They can hide under pepper leaves and sap the strength from the plant. When found indoors, I rinse the aphids off with water under the faucet in the sink.

# REPURPOSED AQUARIUM

Watercress (*Nasturtium officinale*) is used mainly for salads and likes to be grown in shady, wet areas. The leaves have a peppery flavor and are high in vitamins A, C, and K. It tastes best before the plant begins to produce flowers. It is a popular edible in the United Kingdom, but has a short shelf life when sold in the store.

Unlike any other project in this book, this project endorses the use of a container *without* drainage holes! This crop grows best in wet areas, so repurposing a small aquarium will provide a manageable way to grow it and provide it the conditions it will thrive in. The plant does best in very damp soil, so you can mix compost and vermiculite into your potting soil mix to create a blend that will hold onto the moisture the plant craves. The basics of building a terrarium plays into this project, with the use of a charcoal layer above the stone layer. The charcoal with the stone layer helps filter the water present at the bottom of the aquarium.

## WHAT YOU'LL NEED

- A SMALL AQUARIUM (YOU CAN USE A SMALL FISH BOWL–STYLE OR A 9- × 6-INCH [23 × 15 CM] RECTANGULAR ONE.)
- SMALL STONES, SUCH AS PEA GRAVEL
- CHARCOAL
- POTTING SOIL
- COMPOST
- VERMICULITE
- WATERCRESS SEEDS OR PLANTS

## THE STEPS:

**1** | Clean your aquarium with warm soapy water. Allow to dry.

**2** | Add a layer of small stones to the bottom of your aquarium. Follow this with a thin layer of charcoal.

**3** | Take 1 part potting soil and mix in 1 part compost and ½ part vermiculite. The soil should be on the denser side. Then, add your soil mixture on top of the stone and charcoal layer.

**4** | Plant some of your watercress seedlings into the soil. I started my watercress in plastic seed cells ahead of time so I could transplant young plants into the aquarium. But you can sow your seeds directly into the aquarium at this point, too.

**5** | Slowly water with a small spout watering can. You can leave a thin layer of water at the bottom.

## USES FOR WATERCRESS

In addition to salads, watercress can be added to the following:

- Fruit juice or smoothies
- Omelets
- Sandwich garnishes
- Pesto

## HOW TO CARE FOR YOUR WATERCRESS

You can begin harvesting watercress when the stems begin to grow out of your aquarium. Use scissors to make clean cuts right above the leaf nodes to encourage branching.

Getting more plants from your original one is easy, too. You may notice roots growing on the stems—you can snip these stems and place in a small vase of water to encourage the roots to grow longer and then plant them in a new pot.

Watercress is a plant that likes to grow along sources of water, such as creeks, so to grow it successfully, you will want to keep its roots wet. It can be grown in full sun if provided enough water, or part shade.

When growing outdoors, place the aquarium planter in an area where it will be protected from heavy rain. Since the aquarium does not have drainage, it could capture too much water and flood the plant. Keeping your watercress indoors is easy, too. Place it in a sunny window or under a grow light. Water when the water level in the layer of stones has lowered.

# WINDOW BOX VEGGIES

> THIS IS A WARM-SEASON PROJECT THAT CAN BE GROWN OUTDOORS.

## WHAT YOU'LL NEED

- WINDOW BOX (LOOK FOR ONE THAT IS BETWEEN 23 INCHES AND 32 INCHES [58.5–81.5 CM] IN LENGTH.)
- WINDOW BOX BRACKETS (IF NEEDED)
- POTTING SOIL
- PERLITE
- THREE TO FOUR MINIATURE TOMATO PLANTS (DEPENDING ON THE LENGTH OF THE WINDOW BOX)
- DWARF CUCUMBER SEEDS
- MINI BASIL PLANTS

Window box displays do not need to be filled with ornamental plants. Make use of that available growing area by skipping the annual flowers and instead filling it with edibles that will produce food throughout the growing season. This project takes micro varieties of tomatoes and pairs it with a dwarf cucumber variety. Miniature basil is used as a flavorful accent plant.

Do not worry: you do not necessarily need a window to mount a window box underneath! Window boxes can be multipurpose planters that can be used on deck railings, patio walls, and porch railings. See the project sidebar on page 84 on the different types of window boxes you can use.

## THE STEPS:

**1** | Blend 1 part perlite to 2 parts potting soil. (This is to help improve drainage and airflow.)

**2** | Envision a front and back row for your window box. Along the back row, plant your tomato plants along the length of the box, leaving space in between each plant. (See the project sidebar on page 85 on growing miniature tomatoes for guidance.)

**3** | Plant your basil seedlings in the front row, center.

**4** | On either side of the basil, plant your cucumber seeds directly into the window box. You can sow one or two extra seeds and thin after they sprout, if needed. For a small window box, you only need one cucumber plant on either side of the basil. In a slightly longer window box, you can fit two plants on each side.

**5** | Water your window box and set it in a sunny location.

## TYPES OF WINDOW BOXES

There are many choices for window boxes—here are the most common types to choose from.

**Self-watering:** These window boxes include a reservoir to hold excess water underneath the plants. Over time, the water is absorbed back into the soil.

**Plastic:** These window boxes are standard and affordable. You may need to drill drainage holes into the bottom of the plastic and provide a thin layer of stones to help with drainage.

**Hayrack:** This often uses an iron form with a coconut coir lining.

**Wood:** These window boxes can be stained or painted.

# GROWING MINIATURE TOMATOES

• • •

Tomatoes (*Lycopersicon esculentum*) are a warm-season edible. One of the first edible crops I grew with my family were indeterminate tomatoes—the types that can grow 4 to 6 feet (1.2 to 1.8 m) high. Thankfully, over the years, plant breeders have developed varieties that grow in micro form—some only 6 to 8 inches (15–20.5 cm) tall!

As with other micro food varieties, the best selection for miniature tomatoes comes from seed catalogs. There's a tomato for every possible container—whether you are looking for a hanging basket, window box, or a smaller decorative pot.

Tomatoes can be started from seed indoors under a grow light 6 to 8 weeks before your last average frost. Follow the package directions for recommended sowing depth. I like to sow extra seeds to ensure I have enough plants for my own uses.

Micro tomatoes can be grown in small pots.

When the tomato plant reaches about 4 inches (10 cm) high, you can transplant it into a larger container (if your final container destination is not yet available) or directly into the container you wish to use if the temperatures outside are agreeable.

You'll need to harden off your tomatoes before you keep them outside. Hardening off usually takes about a week. During this time, you gradually increase the plant's exposure to outside temperatures and light levels. Place the plant in a protected shady area, beginning with one or two hours on the first day and gradually increasing the hours outside as the week progresses. By the end of the week—as long as there are no frosts and overnight temperatures stay in the 50–55°F (10–13°C) range, you can leave the plants outside to grow. If a late-season frost is in the forecast, bring your plants indoors.

When planting your tomato in its final container, if it is a hanging basket variety, you can remove the lower leaves of the plant and lay the stem horizontally across the soil, allowing it to curve up at one end. The plant will grow roots along the covered stem. For micro varieties that will remain small, this step is not necessary.

Tomatoes need at least 6 hours of sun a day to form fruit. You can fertilize your tomato plants throughout the growing season, but stay away from fertilizers that are high in nitrogen—this will produce a lot of leafy growth but less fruit. Be consistent with watering to prevent calcium deficiencies, which can lead to blossom-end rot in tomatoes. When watering plants, aim to water at the soil line and not the foliage, especially in humid weather. Keeping the leaves dry while watering is the best step you can take to keeping the plants disease-free during the growing season.

Here are three very miniature varieties I like:

- 'Orange Hat' tomato
- 'Mohamed' tomato
- 'Hahms Gelbe' tomato

# WINE BOX SPICE
# AND HERB GARDEN

> THIS IS A WARM-SEASON
> PROJECT THAT CAN BE
> GROWN OUTDOORS.

## WHAT YOU'LL NEED

- WOODEN WINE BOX SIZED FOR 6 BOTTLES (MEASURING APPROXIMATELY 13 × 11 × 7 INCHES [33 × 28 × 18 CM])
- SAFETY GLASSES
- POWER DRILL
- ⅛-INCH (3.2 MM) DRILL BIT
- ⁷⁄₃₂-INCH (5.6 MM) DRILL BIT
- HAMMER
- (4) 1-INCH (2.5 CM) PANELING NAILS; ADDITIONAL (12) 1-INCH PANELING NAILS, IF NECESSARY
- 6 INSIDE-CORNER BRACES AND SCREWS, 1½ INCH (4 CM), WITH ¼-INCH (6 MM) SCREWS
- WOOD GLUE
- DISPOSABLE GLOVES
- (2) 2-GALLON (7.6 L), BPA-FREE PLASTIC FOOD STORAGE BAGS
- SCISSORS
- SMALL STONES, SUCH AS PEA GRAVEL
- POTTING SOIL
- ½ CUP (115 G) OF WORM CASTINGS
- MICRO PEPPER PLANT (SEE THE CHART ON PAGE 90 FOR SUGGESTIONS.)
- THAI BASIL PLANT
- OREGANO PLANT

Wooden wine crates are a great way to disguise items that need to be stored in your home. But why relegate wine boxes to storage only? This project shows off both the container and the plants.

I decided to grow a dwarf cayenne pepper with Thai basil and oregano for my container combo, which can be used in a variety of meals. See the chart on page 90 for other pepper varieties that can be used for spices and are micro friendly.

This project blends companion planting with a handy way to grow herb and spice plants for your garden. By repurposing a wooden wine box into a planter, you'll have a container garden that fits easily on a balcony terrace or back step. When selecting your wine box, I like ones that can hold six bottles because it will fit in a small space.

When preparing your container, you will need to line the inside portion of the wine box with plastic to prevent the wood from warping when you water the plant. Without the liner, the wooden box will absorb water and bow. It's also important to look at the details of how your wine box was created. Is the wine box held together by nails? If yes, you can skip the first step below. If the wine box is created with dovetail joints, you'll need to reinforce the wooden box with nails to provide extra strength and durability.

## THE STEPS:

**1** | If your wine box is not nailed together (dovetail box): Turn the wine box upside down. Wearing your safety glasses, predrill a hole in each corner using the 1/8-inch (3.2 mm) drill bit. Use a hammer to secure a nail in each corner.

**2** | Turn the box right-side up. If your wine box does not have nails to reinforce the siding, you can add them now. On each long side, predrill three holes vertically (at 1 inch, 3½ inches, and 6 inches [at 2.5 cm, 9 cm, and 15 cm]) and then use your hammer to insert nails (for a total of twelve).

**3** | Using the 7/32-inch (5.6 mm) drill bit, drill six evenly spaced drainage holes into the bottom of the wine box.

**4** | Inside your wine box, install four corner braces for additional reinforcement.

**5** | In addition, two of the braces will be installed along the bottom center seam for extra stability.

**6** | Wearing disposable gloves, apply wood glue to the seams of the box. Allow to dry.

**7** | Take the two plastic bags and cut them along the long seams. Unfold the bags so you have two long plastic sheets. Arrange one lengthwise across the inside of the box and one across the width. Use a hammer and a spare nail to puncture holes into the plastic layer that line up with the drainage holes.

There should be extra plastic at the top. For now, drape that over the side.

**8** | Fill your wine box with a layer of small stones about 1 inch (2.5 cm) high. Blend your potting soil and worm castings together and layer on top of the stones, filling the box halfway with the soil blend.

**9** | Plant your pepper, basil, and oregano plant, leaving an equal amount of space between all three plants. Fill in the wine box with more potting soil, leaving about 1 inch (2.5 cm) from the top. Trim the plastic liners so they fall slightly below the edge of the box. Water your plants and set in a sunny spot.

## PEPPERS USED FOR SPICES

◆ ◆ ◆

The spice level of peppers is rated on the Scoville Heat Scale, which measures a chili pepper's pungency and heat in Scoville Heat Units (SHU). Values range from 0 SHU for a green bell pepper to over 2.2 million SHU for a Carolina Reaper chili pepper.

There are many types of peppers that can be used as spices, but these pepper varieties come in micro edible-friendly options (around 18–20 inches [46–51 cm]).

| TYPE OF PEPPER | DESCRIPTION | USE | SCOVILLE RATING (in Scoville Heat Units [SHU]) |
|---|---|---|---|
| CAYENNE PEPPER (*Capsicum annuum*) | Slender, tapered peppers | When dried, it can be used to make cayenne pepper. | 30,000–50,000 SHU |
| JALAPEÑO PEPPER (*Capsicum annuum*) | Green | When dried, this pepper is called chipotle, which can be used to make sauces. | 3,500–8,000 SHU |
| MIRASOL CHILE PEPPER (*Capsicum annuum*) | Red to dark red peppers that grow upright | When dried, they are referred to as *guajillo*. | 2,500–5,000 SHU |
| CHIMAYO PEPPER (*Capsicum annuum*) | Red peppers | These can be dried and used for seasoning. | 4,000–5,000 SHU |
| THAI HOT PEPPER (*Capsicum frutescens*) | Grow upright and mature from green to red | These can be dried and used for red pepper flakes. | 50,000–100,000 SHU |

# TASTE OF ITALY

▶ **THIS IS A WARM-SEASON PROJECT THAT CAN BE GROWN OUTDOORS.**

Grow your own pizza toppings with this combo. Bell peppers, eggplant, cherry tomatoes, oregano, and basil are all key ingredients—either for sauce or for toppings. Basil is a flavorful herb that is also a beneficial companion for all three veggies. There are many great miniature varieties of basil you can use, or you can reign in taller varieties by pinching the stems regularly to make them more compact.

When selecting your plants for this combination, choose varieties that will not shade the other two out. A tomato plant labeled as ideal for hanging baskets is a good choice because it will yield a good number of tomatoes and some stems can arch over the urn's edge. I added oregano to my container planting because the plant grows low and covers the exposed soil. Oregano can be cut and dried and used as an ingredient in tomato sauce.

Pick a sunny spot for this grouping and be sure to water regularly. I opted to use a plastic urn planter for this project in order to house all five plants comfortably. It easily fits along a front walkway or a small courtyard patio.

## WHAT YOU'LL NEED

- URN CONTAINER: 16-INCH (41 CM) DIAMETER; 10 INCHES (25.5 CM) DEEP (NOT INCLUDING THE HEIGHT OF THE BASE)
- CRUSHED STONE
- POTTING SOIL
- COMPOST
- 1 TOMATO PLANT (HANGING BASKET VARIETY)
- 1 MINI PEPPER PLANT
- 1 DWARF EGGPLANT
- 1 OREGANO PLANT
- 1 BASIL PLANT

## THE STEPS:

**1** | Take your container and apply a layer of crushed stone at the bottom (about ½ inch [1.5 cm] to 1 inch [2.5 cm] thick). Mix together 3 parts potting soil and 1 part compost and add to your container, filling halfway.

**2** | Envision your planter with the eggplant, pepper, and tomato forming a triangle design. Take your tomato plant and remove the bottom leaves from the stem. (You can pinch these off or trim with pruners.) Lay the stem horizontally down in the container (the "base" of the triangle), so that it naturally curves upward toward an edge of the container (one "point" of the triangle). When you cover this stem with soil, roots will grow along the stem. This gives the plant extra stability as it grows.

**3** | With the triangle design still in mind, plant your pepper plant in an opposite corner. Follow with the eggplant in the last corner. The points do not to be exact, but serve as a visual guideline for how much space to leave between the plants.

**4** | In the spot between the tomato and the pepper, you can plant the oregano plant. In the spot between the eggplant and the pepper, you can plant the basil plant. As the herbs grow in, they will help shade the soil, which comes in handy, especially around the eggplant's base.

**5** | Fill in soil so the surface is level, leaving about 1 inch (2.5 cm) from the container's top.

### GOOD NEIGHBORS

Growing dwarf varieties of peppers, eggplants, and tomatoes together can be done successfully if you water often. Being inconsistent with watering can stress the plants because they are all heavy feeders. Overwatering can be an issue as well because the nutrients will be depleted more quickly. Signs that your plants might be feeling a little stressed include yellowing leaves or actual wilting. Feeding your plants with an organic, seaweed-based fertilizer will help deliver the nutrients that the plants are looking for.

## GROWING MINI EGGPLANTS

Traditional eggplant (*Solanum melongena*) varieties can take up a lot of space in the garden, which is why I was so happy when dwarf versions became available for the home gardener. The plants are not only compact in size—the fruits are pretty, too. You can grow varieties labeled as "dwarf" or "for containers" in their own pots, or you can combine them with other plants if your container is large enough.

To keep your eggplant happy, you'll want to water it regularly but let the soil dry slightly in between watering. Flea beetles and Colorado Potato Beetles may go after the foliage of your plants. Diatomaceous earth can be applied in a thin layer on the leaves in the early morning hours if flea beetles are particularly bad. For Colorado Potato Beetles, I knock them into a cup of soapy water (the same treatment for Japanese beetles). The neighborhood squirrels and chipmunks like to sample my eggplants, so after the flower sets fruit, I cover my plants with a floating row cover to discourage nibbling—and stealing.

The best time to harvest eggplant is when the fruit is still glossy. If the skin becomes dull, that's a sign that the fruit is overripe and may be bitter or extra seedy. When cutting the fruit off the plant, use a sharp knife or pruners and cut a short piece of the stem at the top. And similar to peas, the more you harvest, the more the plant will continue to grow new fruit.

**PLANT VARIETIES TO TRY:** There are many to choose from, but here are some that I've used in my project:

- Hanging basket varieties of tomatoes: 'Litt'l Bites Cherry'; 'Whippersnapper'
- 'Little Prince' eggplant
- 'Redskin Patio Bell' pepper; 'Pizza My Heart' bell pepper

# MELON MAGIC TRELLIS

> THIS IS A WARM-SEASON PROJECT THAT CAN BE GROWN OUTDOORS.

## WHAT YOU'LL NEED

- MEASURING TAPE
- MARKER
- SAFETY GLASSES
- WORK GLOVES
- (2) ½-INCH (1.5 CM) × 5-FOOT (1.5 M) PVC PIPES
- (3) ½-INCH (1.5 CM) × 2-FOOT (61 CM) PVC PIPES
- PVC PIPE CUTTER
- (2) ½-INCH (1.5 CM)-DIAMETER ELBOW PVC FITTINGS
- (6) ½-INCH (1.5 CM)-DIAMETER TEE PVC FITTINGS
- CHICKEN WIRE ROLL, 4 FEET (1.2 M) IN LENGTH
- WIRE CUTTERS
- 12 PLASTIC ZIP TIES
- (1) 5-GALLON (19 L) FABRIC POT
- POTTING SOIL
- COMPOST
- MELON OR WATERMELON SEEDLINGS

Are you short on space but have a desire to grow sweet-tasting melons? No worries—you do not need a quarter acre (1012 m²) with space for rambling vines to get the flavor kick you desire. Growing melons (*Cucumis melo*) and watermelons (*Citrullus lanatus*) in a compact space is definitely possible if you think vertically.

When shopping for seeds or plants, look for a variety with a description advertising a "compact growing habit" or "suitable for growing in containers." These smaller vines often produce petite fruit—sometimes described as individual servings.

This project utilizes a 5-gallon (19 L) fabric pot and a do-it-yourself, ladder-like trellis that you can assemble using PVC pipes. Layer the PVC pipes with chicken wire to provide ample space for the vine to grow upward. Since both melons and watermelons adore the sunshine, the best spot to set this project up in a south-facing location. The trellis is lightweight and can be leaned against an outdoor wall—minimizing the need for attaching it permanently.

## THE STEPS:

**1** | Using the measuring tape, measure and mark four 15-inch (38 cm) segments on the two 5-foot (1.5 m) PVC pipes. Put on your safety glasses and work gloves and use the PVC pipe cutter to cut the PVC pipe along the markings. You will have eight pieces total after cutting.

**2** | Take the 2-foot (61 cm) PVC pipes and use the PVC pipe cutter to cut each pipe into two 12-inch (30.5 cm) pieces. Starting at what will be the top of the trellis, take the two elbow fittings and attach one to each end of a 12-inch (30.5 cm) PVC pipe. On each elbow, attach one of the 15-inch (38 cm) PVC pieces you previously cut.

**3** | Attach a tee fitting to each 15-inch (38 cm) piece. You can add a 12-inch (30.5 cm) pipe to connect the two. The trellis should start resembling a ladder.

**4** | Continue to connect the remaining tee pieces, attaching the 15-inch (38 cm) PVC pieces vertically and the 12-inch (30.5 cm) PVC pipes horizontally, to the ladder trellis you are creating. When all the pieces are assembled, you will have two "legs" that can be inserted into the soil.

**5** | Take your chicken wire and unroll it so it covers the ladder shape. You will want to leave about 2 inches (5 cm) of chicken wire on either side of the trellis for you to bend and attach it. Cut your wire off the roll.

**6** | Using the zip ties, attach the chicken wire to the PVC frame (six zip ties per side). Carefully fold the open chicken wire closed to prevent sharp edges along the frame.

**7** | Fill your fabric pot with potting soil and compost. For 2 parts potting soil, add ½ part compost.

**8** | Sow three melon seeds into the fabric pot and cover with soil. (You will eventually thin this to one.) If you have a seedling, you could also transplant it directly into the fabric pot. Be careful not to disturb the roots.

**9** | Move your fabric pot to a sunny spot against a wall, leaving a minimum of 12 inches (30.5 cm) and a maximum of 20 inches (51 cm) between the wall and the fabric pot. Insert your trellis into the fabric pot.

**10** | Water well along the soil line, avoiding the leaves if possible.

## GROW MELONS WITH SUCCESS

When given full sun and support, dwarf varieties of melons can be trained to grow vertically and will do so happily. Keep an eye on the soil—you want to keep the plant consistently moist. Adding compost to the soil blend will help with retaining moisture and will provide nutrients to the plant as well. For best results, I grow one plant per 5-gallon (19 L) fabric pot to prevent overcrowding.

Make sure you check your melon plant daily during hot temperatures. The vine will love the heat but needs enough water to help it thrive. Keep soil moist, ideally watering in the morning along the soil line. This will allow the plant time to absorb the water before it quickly evaporates. Try not to expose the plant to watering extremes—steady watering is best.

As the melons begin to form on the trellis, you can use pantyhose to create a sling and tie it to the PVC portions to hold the weight of the fruit as it grows. In fact, if you have critters nearby that like to take a nibble of the melon as it is growing, you can even slip the baby melon *inside* the pantyhose. As the melon grows, the pantyhose will easily expand to accommodate its growth, and it also helps disguise the plant growing inside.

The trick for knowing when to harvest melons for peak flavor is when the stem separates easily from the fruit (also known as *full slip*).

# WORM BUNGALOW

▶ THIS PROJECT IS MEANT
TO BE USED INDOORS.

Raising your own red wiggler worms is a great way to provide steady nutrients for your micro edibles. When you are short on space, the trick is finding a spot to stash them so they are not in the way. Wooden crates found at arts and craft stores can be converted into a storage area to house the worms. Bonus: You can grow one of the several indoor projects on top, such as Pea Shoots (page 160) or the Head Planters (page 122).

This worm bin is designed to be set up indoors in a protected area, such as a garage, attached porch, or in a cool corner of the room. When ordering red wiggler worms, opt for the smallest amount possible or split a larger order with a friend. This project utilizes plastic, shoebox-size containers to house the worms. Once they are set up, they are fairly low maintenance, and you can add food scraps once a week. Because the bin is on the smaller side, if you find that you have a larger quantity of food scraps, you can "level up" and add another storage box on top with larger holes so the worms can pass through the layers freely.

I recommend creating your worm bin before ordering your worms.

## WHAT YOU'LL NEED

- 1 WOODEN STACKING CRATE WITH LID, 12.5 × 9.6 × 17.9 INCHES (32 × 24.5 × 45.5 CM)
- (3) 6-QUART (5.7 L) CONTAINERS, SUCH AS SHOE BOX STORAGE CONTAINERS, 13.6 × 8.3 × 4.8 INCHES (34.5 × 21 × 12 CM) (YOU'LL ONLY NEED ONE LID.)
- SAFETY GLASSES
- POWER DRILL
- 3/32-INCH (2.4 MM) DRILL BIT
- 9/64-INCH (3.6 MM) DRILL BIT
- SMALL INSECT SCREEN MESH
- SCISSORS
- WATER-RESISTANT GLUE
- DISPOSABLE GLOVES
- RED WIGGLER WORMS (FEWER THAN 100)
- SOIL
- SHREDDED NEWSPAPER
- OPTIONAL: PAINT TO DECORATE WOODEN CRATE

## THE STEPS:

**1** | Using the ³⁄₃₂-inch (2.4 mm) drill bit and wearing your safety glasses, take one of the plastic 6-quart (5.7 L) containers and drill a hole for drainage in each corner. Add six more holes along the bottom layer.

**2** | With the container right-side up, with the width facing you, use the ⁹⁄₆₄-inch (3.6 mm) drill bit to drill a larger hole for air about ½ inch (1.5 cm) down from the top's center. Drill eight air holes into the top lid. (Providing enough air holes for the worms is important—a lack of oxygen will cause the worms to try and escape your bin!)

**3** | Cut a small piece of the insect mesh to cover the bottom holes on the plastic shoebox. Wearing disposable gloves, attach the screen mesh with water-resistant glue on the outside of the container and let dry for the recommended time.

**4** | After the glue has cured, take a second 6-quart (5.7 L) container and place your first bin into this one. Allow them to sit loosely on top of each other. The bottom bin will hold any liquid that might drain from your bin.

**5** | Add your worms to the bin with the drilled holes. Follow the directions that come with your red wiggler worms, which can include adding water to rehydrate them (due to shipping). Add some soil and shredded newspaper to your bin and then add your worms. Allow them to get settled for a few days before you begin to add food scraps.

**6** | Take your third container and drill holes in the bottom using the ⁹⁄₆₄-inch (3.6 mm) drill bit. This will be the layer that you encourage the worms to move freely into, to not only maximize your space but help with the composting. Place the third bin into the second bin and attach the lid with the holes on top. Place the three containers into your wooden crate with the lid.

## WHAT IS VERMICOMPOSTING?

Vermicomposting is the breaking down of food materials by worms. The by-products of this include worm castings (which are great additions to soil) and leachate, which is a liquid that is from the worm casting bin that can be further diluted and used to boost plant growth.

## WHY USE RED WIGGLER WORMS
## AND NOT WORMS I FIND IN NATURE?

Red wiggler worms are known for being able to eat and process food scraps. They are easier to distinguish than larger worms due to their smaller size. You can obtain red wiggler worms through reputable businesses that specialize in vermicomposting. Do not purchase larger worms, labeled as nightcrawlers, for this project.

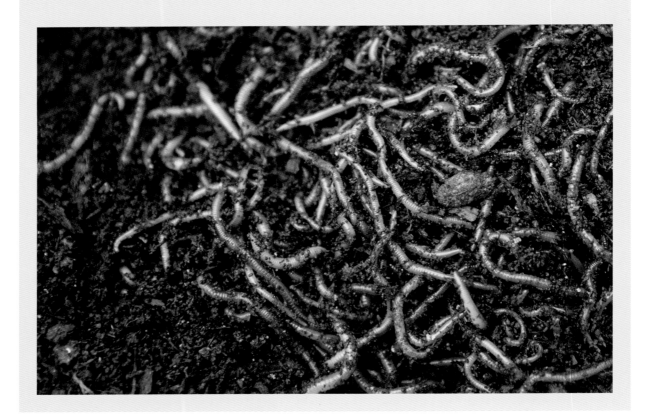

## WHAT CAN I FEED MY WORMS?
## AND OTHER CARE AND MAINTENANCE TIPS

Once set up, worms are fairly low maintenance. They enjoy the dark and do most of their work with the lights out. Since this worm bin project is meant for a small space, you do not need to provide heaping amounts of food waste to feed your worms. Some items I feed my worms included lettuce and berries past their prime or trimmings from root crops.

Worms will happily munch on any of the following: vegetables and fruits, coffee grounds, and loose tea. When adding food scraps to the container, choose one spot to leave food, either in the center of the bin or on the left or right side. You can do this once a week. To prevent fruit flies, make sure you cover your food scraps with soil or shredded newspaper. Usually the moisture from the food is enough to keep the bin from getting too dry, but if your bin seems to be drying out, you can add some wet shredded newspaper to replace the moisture.

Over time, the worms will break down the food and create worm castings. The worm castings can be removed and added to your soil mixtures or used as a top dressing on the soil line of plants. The leachate that drains from the bin can be diluted further with water and used on your plants.

Do not feed the worms any meat leftovers (such as fat and bones) or dairy products. A simple way to remember what not to feed them is to refer to them as vegan worms.

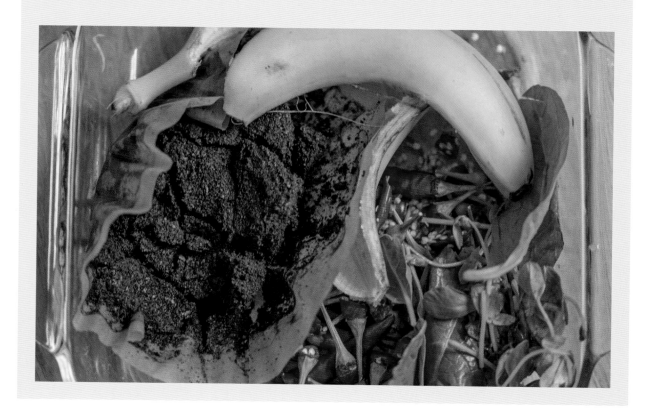

# RAINWATER COLLECTOR WITH LIVING WREATH

Repurposing rainwater for your micro garden does not have to be your rain barrel's only function. You can use the barrel's footprint to grow a mini crop of edibles, too! To make a rain barrel plant-friendly, I fashioned a way to create metal wreath forms into a living wreath that sits on top of the barrel. For this project, I decided to use bush beans as my edible of choice.

This is a two-part project. First, you need to assemble the rain barrel. When searching for a container to collect water in, I checked several online marketplaces. I decided to go with a 60-gallon (227 L) food-grade barrel that was used to store and ship pickled peppers. I liked that the barrel came with a screw-top lid, and I instantly envisioned attaching a fine screen mesh to keep the mosquitoes out. You have the option of adding one or two spigot openings to your rain barrel. One is a hose bib, which can sit about ⅓ to ½ of the way up from the bottom of the barrel. This allows easy access to refilling a watering can. The other option is at the bottom of the barrel. This part can be used to hook up a hose, and all the water will be easier to drain from the barrel. I also added an option for rainwater over-flow. You can link this up to another rain barrel or just use it to divert water away from the house foundation.

When looking for a barrel that will fit your needs, evaluate your available space in proximity to a gutter downspout. You'll also want to check your local neighborhood ordinances to make sure a rain barrel is allowed on your property. (One more tip: If you are diverting a rain gutter to collect water for your barrel, I recommend checking that your gutters are cleared and unclogged. Otherwise, your rain barrel may collect sediment in addition to rain water.)

Using a metal wreath form that is situated to fit around the top opening of the rain barrel, but not on top of the screen opening, means you will not have to worry about soil getting into the barrel.

## PART 1: ASSEMBLING THE RAIN BARREL

## THE STEPS:

1 | Take your rain barrel and decide where you want the hose bib to be. If you are going to elevate your rain barrel on cement blocks, you can place the hose bib lower to the bottom of the barrel. If you are going to set it up without a platform, you can position the hose bib about ⅓ up from the bottom. (Basically, you want it high enough for a watering can to fit underneath.) Mark the spot.

## WHAT YOU'LL NEED

- FOOD-SAFE STORAGE BARREL WITH A SCREW-TOP LID
- MARKER
- SAFETY GLASSES
- POWER DRILL
- ¾-INCH (2 CM) SPADE DRILL BIT
- 4–6 NEOPRENE FENDER WASHERS: 2¼ INCH (6 CM) OUTER DIMENSION; ⅛ INCH (0.5 CM)-THICK
- ¾-INCH (2 CM) BRASS HOSE BIB (FOR WATERING CAN SPOUT)
- CLEAR SILICONE CAULK
- CAULKING GUN
- DISPOSABLE GLOVES
- (2) ¾-INCH (2 CM) MALE × ¾-INCH (2 CM) FEMALE HOSE TO THREADED PIPE CONNECTORS (FOR WATERING CAN SPOUT AND HOSE ATTACHMENT AT THE BOTTOM)
- ¾- × ¾-INCH (2 × 2 CM) 90-DEGREE BRASS ELBOW FITTING (FOR OVERFLOW PORTION)
- ¾-INCH (2 CM) THREADED PIPE TO HOSE CONNECTOR, DOUBLE MALE × ½-INCH (1.5 CM) FEMALE (FOR OVERFLOW PORTION)
- BRASS HOSE END SHUTOFF VALVE
- INSECT SCREEN MESH
- SCISSORS
- OPTIONAL: MOSQUITO DUNK, WHICH IS A DONUT SHAPED TABLET THAT USES *BACILLUS THURINGIENSIS* SUBSP. *ISRAELENSIS* (BTI) TO KILL MOSQUITOS (I FIND THIS A SAFE, NONTOXIC METHOD THAT IS HELPFUL TO KEEP MOSQUITOES FROM BREEDING IN THE STANDING WATER THROUGHOUT THE GROWING SEASON.)

**2** | Put on your safety glasses. Using your spade drill bit, drill into the marked spot. The spade bit makes a nice round hole for your hose bib to be inserted into.

**3** | At this time, you will also want to mark the hole for where the overflow spout will go. This should be near the top of your barrel. You can use the spade bit to drill into this spot, too. If you opt to have a bottom opening where the hose shutoff valve will go, mark the spot and drill that now as well.

**4** | Put on disposable gloves. Take one of the washers and put it around the hose bib. Turn the hose bib clockwise to insert it into the hole. Before it is flush against the rain barrel, apply silicone caulk on the side of the washer that will face the barrel. Turn the hose bib so the washer is flush with the barrel and the hose bib is right-side up.

**5** | Inside the barrel, take another washer where the hose bib is inserted and attach one of the ¾-inch (2 cm) male to female threaded pipe connectors. Apply silicone caulk around the side of the washer that will contact the rain barrel and press against the inside of the barrel to create a seal. Tighten the brass part for a snug fit.

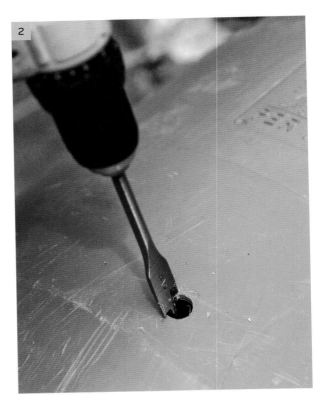

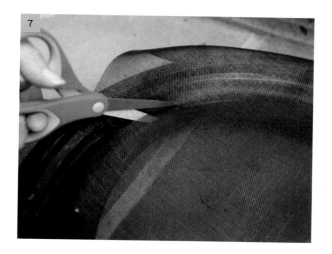

6 | You will follow steps 4 and 5 when adding the overflow valve and the optional hose attachment.

7 | Allow the silicone caulk to dry on all the parts attached to the rain barrel. While it is drying, take the screw-top lid and turn it upside down. Cut the insect mesh so that it is the same size as the inner opening. Apply the silicone caulk to the lid's lip and place the mesh screen on top. While still wearing your disposable gloves, you can smooth the silicone caulk with your fingers so that it evenly distributed.

Once the silicone has dried on all parts, test your rain barrel by filling it with water to ensure that it does not leak. If it does, reapply the silicone to the specific area.

## PART 2: CREATING THE LIVING WREATH

### WHAT YOU'LL NEED

- 2 METAL WREATH FORMS (I USED TWO 20-INCH [51 CM]-DIAMETER FORMS SO IT WOULD FIT AROUND THE TOP OF THE RAIN BARREL OPENING. MEASURE THE DIAMETER OF THE BARREL YOU ARE WORKING WITH AND PURCHASE THE APPROPRIATE SIZE.)
- COCONUT COIR SHEET, MEASURED OUT TO BE 24 × 24 INCHES (61 × 61 CM) TO FIT A 20-INCH (53.5 CM) DIAMETER WREATH FORM
- SCISSORS
- BOX CUTTER
- WORK GLOVES
- (30) 10-INCH (25.5 CM) BROWN PLASTIC ZIP TIES
- POTTING SOIL
- BUSH BEAN SEEDS

### THE STEPS:

1 | Take the coconut coir layer and place one of the wreath forms on top. For the coconut coir on the outer layer of the wreath, measure 3 inches (7.5 cm) out from the entire wreath form and trim off the excess. Wearing work gloves, use the box cutter to cut out the inner circle of the coconut coir (approximately 3 inches [7.5 cm] from the wire form). This will allow you to bend the coconut coir for the next step, so it does not need to be precise cuts.

**2** | Place one of the wreath forms on the table and place the coconut coir layer on top. Then, place the second wreath form on top. Beginning with one side of the outer wreath forms, curve your coconut coir layer so it forms "a wall" between the two wreath forms. Use a zip tie to hold this in place, but secure it loosely. The loosened zip tie will allow you flexibility to bend and shape as you fit the coconut coir layer into the frame. Continue to curve the coir layer and secure with a zip tie every few inches (7.5–10 cm) for half of the wreath.

**3** | Use scissors to provide a cleaner trim of the coconut coir center.

**4** | Next, use zip ties to secure the other half of the wreath forms to the inner wreath circle. Again, loosely tie the zip ties when securing. Curve up the coir layer so it again forms an inside wall and fasten the zip ties as you move around the wreath form. At this point, half of the wreath should look like a long pocket that you can fill with potting soil.

Repeat steps 2 and 4 for the other half of the wreath. When finished, the two wreath forms will be joined together.

**5** | Fill the coconut coir "pocket" with potting soil. Tuck your bush bean seeds into the soil and cover with more soil. You'll want to sow at least six seeds, depending on how large your wreath frame is (for mine, I was able to fit 12 seeds). You can sow extra seeds to improve germination rates, but you will want to thin plants as they grow to allow for enough room for the roots.

**6** | Tighten the zip ties around the wreath so the coconut coir layer is secure. Trim off the excess portions of the zip tie. Water the wreath. Place the wreath on the top of your rain barrel. The bean seeds will emerge within 5–7 days.

# TIPS FOR GROWING BUSH BEANS

Beans (*Phaseolus vulgaris*) are easy to grow and create colorful pods in green, purple, and yellow, adding pops of color to your garden and your meals.

When I think of bean plants, I group them mainly into two categories: pole beans and bush beans. Pole beans can be for snap bean or dry bean production, and bush beans are often snap bean varieties. Snap beans produce crunchy pods that can be eaten right off the vine. For micro edible gardening, you will want to use bush varieties since they do not require large trellising and support. Starting from seed is easy. Beans are a warm weather plant, seeking full sun and warm soil when planted. Look for seeds that offer disease resistance.

In containers, use well-draining soil. Keep the soil moist throughout growing—dried out soil can affect how the plant sets beans. Water at the base to prevent disease spread and accidentally knocking bean flowers off while watering. Avoid fertilizing with a fertilizer with a high nitrogen value—this will result in many pretty green leaves but fewer pods.

Harvest beans by making clean snips along the stems. Similar to garden peas, the more you pick, the more they produce. The size of ripe bean pods varies by plant; check your seed packet for specifics. Pick pods before they overripen on the plant. (Overripening is when the beans become so large that you can feel them through the pod. Of course, that is great if you are growing beans for dry soup beans; but in this case, we're growing snap beans for eating.)

Beans are also great for succession sowing, to ensure a continuous harvest throughout the growing season. You can sow them every two to three weeks in different containers or window boxes. Beans are great gateway plants for kids—which is why the life cycle of a bean plant is often a school lesson! The seeds are easy for little fingers to pick up and plant.

Beans can attract both insect and animal pests. If you live in a spot where wildlife can access your outdoor area, keep your bean plants out of reach of groundhogs and rabbits. While the list of insect pests for beans is long—including aphids, Mexican bean beetles, cucumber beetles, flea beetles, and caterpillars—they are usually easy to manage. Keeping an eye on your plants as they grow will help you catch problems early and prevent outbreaks from happening. Bush beans can be covered with a floating row cover after setting out to discourage beetles or caterpillars. This can be removed when the plants begin to flower so they can be pollinated. Knock aphids off with a stream of water, pop beetles in a cup of soapy water, and handpick caterpillars to control.

# CUKE TOWER

THIS IS A WARM-SEASON PROJECT THAT CAN BE GROWN OUTDOORS.

## WHAT YOU'LL NEED

- 4-INCH (10 CM) × 5-FOOT (1.5 M) PVC PIPE
- ¾-INCH (2 CM) × 3-FOOT (91.5 CM) PVC PIPE
- SAFETY GLASSES
- POWER DRILL
- ⁹/₆₄-INCH (3.6 MM) DRILL BIT
- METAL WALL ANCHOR KIT WITH STEEL WIRE STRAPS (THIS IS IMPORTANT IF YOUR TOWER IS EXPOSED TO WIND, SUCH AS AN APARTMENT BALCONY.)
- 14-INCH (35.5 CM) TERRA-COTTA POT, WITH PLANT SAUCER
- 30–40 POUND (13.6–18 KG) BAG OF SMALL TO MEDIUM SIZE STONES
- POTTING SOIL
- CUCUMBER SEEDS
- DILL SEEDS
- NARROW STRIP OF CHICKEN WIRE THAT JUST COVERS THE LARGE PVC PIPE
- OPTIONAL: STEPLADDER

As a child, I remember hot summer days where meals included cucumber salad—a blend of cucumbers blended with sugar, pepper, and salt and soaked in vinegar. While some cucumber salad recipes call for sour cream and onions, my mom would omit both, and the result would be a refreshing light lunch.

Luckily, cucumbers can be grown in areas where space is at a premium. For this project, I used a large PVC pipe to create a tower where the plant is situated at the top and dangles down. I also added a layer of chicken wire around the pipe when I noticed that the cucumber tendrils were still seeking something to reach out and hold on to.

The tower keeps the cucumbers off the ground, and the fruit is easy to spot for harvesting. I added dill to the bottom pot along with two more cucumber plants that could grow upward as the plants in the top cascaded down, thereby completing the tower look.

This is a two-person project, so enlist your friend or neighbor to help with assembling this one! Find a flat surface to set up your Cuke Tower. Spots to consider include along a walkway or a corner on your balcony.

## THE STEPS:

**1** | Put on your safety glasses. Take your ¾-inch (2 cm) PVC pipe and drill three evenly spaced holes into one side of the pipe. This pipe will deliver water to the roots of the cucumber plant inside the larger PVC pipe.

**2** | This is the time to add the metal wall anchor kit to the tower if you are opting to use it. Follow the directions on the package for using the steel wire to wrap around the pole and then secure the two brackets to the wall.

**3** | Take your 14-inch (35.5 cm)-wide pot (with the saucer underneath) and place the 4-inch (10 cm) PVC pipe in the center. Fill the pot halfway with stones. Top with potting soil, leaving about 1 inch (2.5 cm) from the top.

**4** | Have your helper hold the PVC pipe straight in the center. Add your stones to the center of the PVC pipe until you reach about halfway up. Using a stepladder can make this easier.

**5** | Take your ¾-inch (2 cm) PVC pipe and place it inside the 4-inch (10 cm) PVC pipe. Position it so the holes are facing the center of the pipe. Carefully add potting soil to the center of the pole, leaving about 1½ inches (4 cm) free at the top. You can finish the wall mounting bracket at this time, too.

**6** | Water the soil to help it settle inside the pole. You'll want to start with a slow steady stream—anything faster might cause the water to over-flow, taking your soil with it. (The water will help compact and settle the soil inside the pipe.) Test out the ¾-inch (2 cm) watering tube when you water. You can also water the soil in the pot below as well. At this time, sow your seeds at the top of the tower. You'll want to grow three plants, so you can add up to five seeds at this point to ensure germination. (If all five germinate, you can relo-cate two plants or thin them out.) Cover with soil (following the seed packet recommendation) and water lightly again.

**7** | Cover the pole with the chicken wire. Sow seeds for dill in the bottom pot and cover with soil and water. Depending on outside tempera-ture, your seeds should begin germinating within 5–7 days. Water the tower as needed as the plants grow.

**8** | When the cucumber plants reach about 4 or 5 inches (10 or 13 cm) high, they will natu-rally begin to bend and curve over the top of the tower and begin to cascade downward.

# GROW CRUNCHY CUCUMBERS!

Cucumbers (*Cucumis sativus*) are an easy-to-grow edible, that given the right growing conditions, will happily produce fruit for you. For micro edible projects, choose a cucumber that has a small spread (ideally under 2 feet [61 cm]) and is described as a bush habit instead of a vigorous vine. These cucumber plants will not be as vigorous as their vine-like siblings. The bush varieties will still send out a few tendrils in search of support.

Cucumbers are warm-season crops that are also sun worshippers. I find it easiest to direct sow seeds outside after the danger of frost has passed. There are many different types of cucumbers available to grow—from the long and slender versions to the round and bulky. They can be used for slicing and eating raw or for pickling.

Consistent water is key for growing healthy cucumber plants. In fact, 95% of their weight comes from water! It's no surprise that cucumbers are great for hydration. Cucumbers grown in containers will also need regular feeding. I use a liquid seaweed blended for vegetables (lower nitrogen) when watering. I

use a slightly weaker concentration when watering with my watering can, so that way I can feed them weekly.

If your cucumber plants receive fluctuations in watering, they can yield deformed fruit.

Cucumbers are fairly low maintenance plants, but there are some things to keep an eye out for throughout your growing season. One is powdery mildew, which coats the leaves with a white film. The best way to avoid this is to provide as much air circulation as possible around plants as they grow and to plant varieties that are powdery-mildew resistant. (This will be included on seed packets and sometimes on plant tags.)

Cucumber beetles and squash bugs can be pests. I find that the best prevention is actually direct sowing the seed in the garden once the warm season is already under way. In my area, I am able to minimize the impact of the insects because the plant is not available when their growth cycle begins. You can also cover the plants with a floating row cover from the very beginning, especially in areas where an infestation is bad. For containers, this means you will have to tuck the floating row cover underneath the pot to keep it in place. When the cucumber plants begin to bloom, you can remove the cover so the flowers can be pollinated.

Be sure to check the plants regularly for insect pests and remove them by hand when possible. They move quickly, so you'll need to be fast as well if you are trying to knock them into a cup of soapy water. Check the undersides of leaves for eggs and remove those as well.

# MINI SALSA GARDEN

There are differing opinions on what makes a great salsa recipe, but many can agree that the core ingredients include tomatoes and peppers. A micro tomato variety paired with a dwarf pepper plant can be combined in one container for this project. Cilantro is an herb that is often used in Mexican dishes and can also be paired in this planter. When choosing a tomato, look for a high-yielding compact cherry plant that is labeled for "growing in containers."

Tomatoes and peppers are heavy feeders, so blending in some compost to your soil mixture will help give them the nutrient boost to get going. When blending the soils, do not be too heavy handed with the compost—it can compact the soil in containers if there is too much. Continue to feed them with a liquid seaweed fertilizer meant for vegetables throughout the growing season.

All you'll need at the grocery store is an onion, salt, and lime juice, and you will be good to go in creating your own homemade salsa.

## WHAT YOU'LL NEED

- DECORATIVE GLAZED POTTERY: 12 INCHES (30.5 CM) IN DIAMETER; 8 INCHES DEEP (30.5 CM BY 20.5 CM)
- SMALL STONES, SUCH AS PEA GRAVEL, FOR DRAINAGE
- POTTING SOIL
- COMPOST
- MICRO TOMATO VARIETY
- PEPPER VARIETY—YOUR CHOICE OF JALAPEÑO OR BELL
- CILANTRO SEEDS

## THE STEPS:

**1** | Add 1 inch (2.5 cm) layer of small stones to the bottom of your pot. Combine your potting soil with your compost. For 2 parts potting soil, add ½ part compost.

**2** | Plant your tomato on one side of the pot and your pepper plant on the opposite side.

**3** | In the space in between both plants, sow your cilantro seeds. (See the project sidebar on opposite page for cilantro growing tips.) You can also purchase cilantro seedlings at your garden center and transplant them into the container at this stage.

**4** | Fill in the pot with the remaining soil and water. Place your Salsa Garden in full sun.

The Salsa Garden is small enough that you can use it as a table centerpiece or as a housewarming gift.

## PICK YOUR PEPPER— JALAPEÑO OR BELL

Peppers (*Capsicum annuum*) have different heat intensities. Deciding if you want to use a jalapeño or a bell pepper in your planter really comes down to your flavor choice. Do you want to create a hotter salsa or a milder one? Bell peppers do not have heat, while jalapeños do.

Jalapeño peppers add heat to recipes.

## GROW GREAT CILANTRO

Cilantro (*Coriandrum sativum*) is an herb that can be grown from seed. Cilantro is the same as coriander—except coriander is the seed part of cilantro that is used as a spice in cooking. Cilantro leaves are often used to season dishes.

To increase its germination rate, you can soak the seeds in water for 24 hours before planting them. You can sow cilantro seeds directly into your planter or start it ahead of time and transplant in as a seedling (just like you would do with the tomato and pepper plant in this project). As the tomato and pepper plant grow, they will provide some shade to the cilantro. (Cilantro can bolt if the growing temperature is too hot.)

To harvest cilantro, use clean scissors to cut sprigs from the plant.

Cilantro is an herb that can be succession sown throughout the season.

# CHERRY TOMATO CANDY

> THIS IS A WARM-SEASON PROJECT THAT CAN BE GROWN OUTDOORS.

## WHAT YOU'LL NEED

- SAFETY GLASSES
- TOWEL
- 1-GALLON (3.8 L) GLASS STORAGE JAR, WITHOUT THE LID (I USED A PENNY CANDY–STYLE JAR.)
- TAPE (MASKING OR BLUE PAINTER'S TAPE)
- POWER DRILL
- ½-INCH (1.27 CM) DIAMOND DRILL BIT
- WATERING CAN WITH COLD WATER
- SMALL STONES, SUCH AS PEA GRAVEL, AND ONE MEDIUM SIZE STONE TO COVER THE DRAINAGE HOLE
- POTTING SOIL
- MICRO TOMATO PLANT OR HANGING BASKET PLANT VARIETY

Cherry tomatoes are bite-sized and a delicious treat on a hot day. Snacking on them is what gave me this project idea. What if you had tomatoes growing in an iconic candy jar? You can use a micro variety of tomatoes for this project or a dwarf hanging basket variety.

This project is the perfect size to fit on an outdoor patio wall or table. Tomatoes thrive in full sun, but you will want to keep an eye on the moisture level of the soil since the glass can dry out the soil a bit faster. But—on the plus side—it will be easy to see when the soil is dry and in need of a boost. You can also fertilize throughout the season.

The trick with the project is drilling into glass. It is a similar process to drilling a ceramic coffee mug (see page 49), but it will take a bit longer because you need to use your drill at the lowest setting and add water to keep the drill bit and glass from overheating and breaking.

## THE STEPS:

1 | Put on your safety glasses. Lay your towel on the table and place the glass storage jar on top, upside down. Place a small piece of masking or painter's tape at the bottom where you want to drill your hole for drainage.

2 | Position your drill at a 45-degree angle and on a slow speed, begin to mark the tape on the glass. You'll only want to scratch the glass at this point in order to give the drill bit something to catch as you continue to drill.

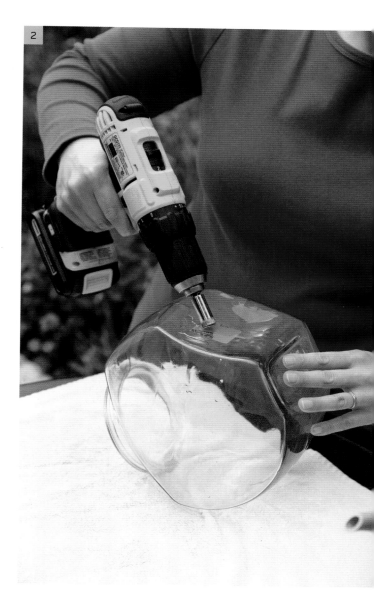

**3** | Once your glass is scratched, remove the tape. On the lowest setting for your hand drill, position your drill at a 45-degree angle and continue to drill. Stop periodically as you drill to add cold water to the spot where you are drilling the hole. (This is to prevent the glass from overheating and cracking.)

**4** | As you continue to (slowly) drill, move your hand so you gradually move from a 45-degree angle to a 90-degree angle. Continue to stop and add water to the surface as needed.

**5** | Once at a 90-degree angle, continue to drill at a slow speed. Do not use your weight to push into the glass jar (the extra force could crack it when the drill makes the final cut for the hole).

**6** | Once the hole is created in the glass, carefully remove your drill bit from the hole by reversing the direction of the drill bit and slowly running it until it is removed. Use a piece of tape to remove any loose shards of glass from the hole.

**7** | Turn the jar right-side up. Add the medium-size stone to cover the drainage hole and add smaller stones in a thin layer along the bottom. Next, add your potting soil mix, filling up the jar about ⅓ of the way. The jar is angled so the soil will be angled, too.

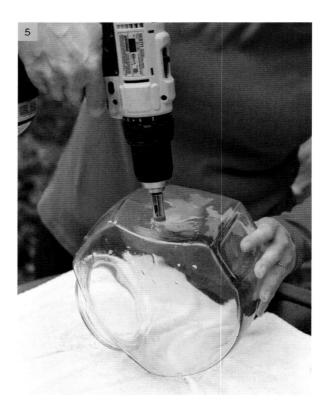

**PLANT VARIETIES TO TRY:** The best type of tomatoes for this project include varieties that are labeled for growing in hanging baskets. These stems will naturally curve and support tresses of tomatoes, which is the same shape the plant in the candy jar will take.

**8** | Take your tomato plant, remove any of the lower leaves along the stem, and lay it horizontally into the jar. You'll want to cover the stem with the potting soil. Fill it up so the soil is about ½ inch (1.5 cm) below the mouth of the jar. Water your plant.

**9** | Place the plant in a protected but sunny spot. You can place this on a patio ledge or a table, to allow the tomato to grow and cascade as it grows. Check it daily during warm weather to make sure it does not dry out.

> THIS IS BOTH A COOL- AND WARM-SEASON PROJECT THAT CAN BE GROWN INDOORS OR OUTDOORS.

## WHAT YOU'LL NEED

- HEAD PLANTER
- SMALL STONES, SUCH AS PEA GRAVEL
- POTTING SOIL
- SEEDS OR YOUNG PLANTS

Express your creativity and individuality by finding funky head planters to grow micro edibles. Think chives crew cuts, kale waves, or a head full of baby greens. Dwarf varieties of herbs such as oregano and dill can also be used for creative hairstyling.

Head planters can be found online, in plant nurseries, or boutique shops. The key to making head planters look like real hairstyles is in the upkeep. Just how bonsai artists perfect their miniature trees, if you wish to have your head planter serve a dual purpose of being on display and available for meals or garnishes, be thoughtful in where you snip.

Ideally, you will want to use a head planter that includes a drainage hole. Depending on the material, you may be able to drill a hole if it does not feature one. If drilling a hole is not possible, use a smaller plastic pot that can be inserted into the head planter and lifted out and removed when watering is needed.

To complete the look, you can also add accessories to your head planters, such as sunglasses or clip-on earrings.

## THE STEPS:

Planting your head planter is easy! Add a thin layer of small stones. Next, add your potting soil. Make a hole in the center of the pot and add your plant. Fill the pot with soil so it is level and then water. You can start by sowing seeds and thinning the plants as they grow. Or, you can start with a young seedling. The size of your container ties into what you can grow. (See the project sidebar on page 124.)

### GROWING TIP

The best time to trim your edible plants for looks is when you are ready to use it as an ingredient in a meal.

## EDIBLE LOCKS

| PLANT | CHARACTERISTICS | HOW MANY |
|---|---|---|
| KALE (*Brassica oleracea*) | Look for a multi-colored seed mixture that can provide green and purple "waves." | Grow either baby greens or one dwarf plant. |
| SWISS CHARD (*Beta vulgaris*) | Look for a colorful variety to help stand out from across the room. | Start out with a handful of seeds and thin as they grow. You'll want to be left with one or two plants. |
| MINT (*Mentha spp.*) | Varieties offer different looks, but most will provide "long locks" from the runners the plant sends out. (Trim to keep it in control.) | One plant will do! |
| CHIVES (*Allium schoenoprasum*) | Leave it long for a windswept look or cut it back for a crew cut. | A potted plant from the store works for a head start, or you can start several seeds in the planter. |
| NASTURTIUM (*Tropaeolum minus*) | Mounding varieties work well, and flowers add accent colors. | One plant will fill it out nicely. |

Head planters can be grouped together or act as a conversation piece on their own. Pay attention to the plant's light needs when deciding the best place to display your head planter.

# THYME CHESSBOARD

> THIS IS A WARM-SEASON PROJECT THAT CAN BE GROWN OUTDOORS.

## WHAT YOU'LL NEED

- 14-INCH (35.5 CM) SQUARE CAKE PAN
- SAFETY GLASSES
- POWER DRILL
- 3/32-INCH (2.4 MM) DRILL BIT
- SMALL STONES, SUCH AS PEA GRAVEL
- POTTING SOIL
- WOODEN SKEWERS (YOU CAN FIND THEM AT THE GROCERY STORE.)
- 34 THYME PLANTS (I USED *THYMUS PRAECOX*.)
- (33) 1½-INCH (4 CM) WOODEN SQUARE PIECES (CHECK CRAFT STORES OR ONLINE HANDMADE CRAFT SHOPS), PAINTED TO YOUR COLOR CHOICE

This project is great for a table centerpiece and grows thyme in a unique way. Sure to be a conversation piece, the Thyme Chessboard is based on the blueprint of an actual chessboard, which measures out 64 squares in an 8 × 8 square grid. I used thyme grown from seed to get more plants—for only the cost for a seed packet.

Thyme is a slow grower, so this is a good addition to your seed starting repertoire early in the growing season. Once the plants form small "clumps," they are ready for transplanting into the cake pan for this project. To keep the board looking it's best, you will need to periodically snip the plant back. You can use your cuttings to flavor soups and meat dishes, as well as egg dishes. I froze my cuttings in small plastic bags with a little water so they could be added to soups and stews at a later date. You can also dry the herbs for storage.

## THE STEPS:

**1** | Turn your cake pan upside down. Wearing your safety glasses, drill evenly spaced holes for drainage. (I drilled 16 holes.)

**2** | Flip your pan right-side up and add a thin layer of small stones and then a layer of potting soil.

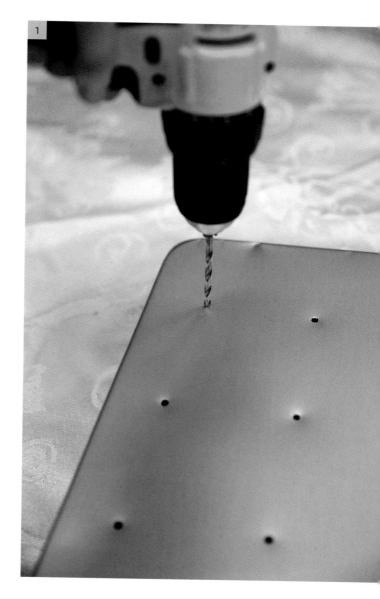

**3** | Measure out 8 rows on the length and width of your cake pan. This will give you 64 squares, with each square measuring approximately 1.8 inches (4.5 cm). Use wooden skewers to create a chessboard pattern.

**4** | Beginning at the top left corner of the pan, take your thyme plants and plant them in every other square. Then, place your wooden squares in every other spot, so a checkerboard pattern appears. Remove the wooden skewers. Water with a sprinkler head attachment on your watering can.

**5** | Trim your thyme plants so they fit neatly within their squares. To encourage compact growth, trim your thyme right above the leaf nodes.

# HOW TO GROW THYME FROM SEED
## (AND AFTER CARE)

Thyme takes a bit of time to grow from seed, but with enough patience, it is worth the wait. You get many plants for the cost of a seed packet!

For this project, I opted to use creeping thyme (*Thymus praecox*) because it stays 6 to 10 inches (15–25.5 cm) tall. I start my seed very early in the growing season by surface sowing the seed. It can be slow to sprout, taking between 10 to 30 days. I also add bottom heat to my seed tray with a seed heat mat, which seems to speed up germination.

When the plant has two sets of true leaves, the plant begins to grow much faster. I transplanted mine when it was about 1 inch (2.5 cm) high and wide.

Thyme is a low-water user, which makes it ideal for this project. I let the soil dry out between watering. It does not like to be wet for long periods, so choose a well-draining potting soil blend.

# SHADY GARDEN BED

> **THIS IS BOTH A COOL- AND WARM-SEASON PROJECT THAT CAN BE GROWN OUTDOORS.**

For a literal take on a garden bed, look no further. This portable garden project is for everyone who desires more sunlight but has to deal with shady growing conditions. Leafy greens will tolerate partial shade conditions, especially during the warm season. The plants will grow a bit slower in partial shade than if they were in full sun.

You can also swap out the contents of the garden bed depending on which season you are in. For a cool season, try growing spinach, lettuce, kale, or arugula. For the warm season, try growing chard.

This is a multiday project. You'll start with spray painting the wooden doll bed and letting the paint dry for the recommended time, which is usually 24 hours. The next day, you can attach the chicken wire and coconut coir layer to begin planting.

## WHAT YOU'LL NEED

- WOODEN DOLL BED
- SPRAY PAINT
- MASK
- SAFETY GLASSES
- DISPOSABLE GLOVES
- CHICKEN WIRE
- COCONUT COIR SHEET (I STARTED WITH A 20- × 20-INCH [51 × 51 CM] PIECE AND TRIMMED IT TO FIT.)
- WIRE CUTTERS
- WORK GLOVES
- SCISSORS
- STAPLE GUN
- POTTING SOIL
- YOUNG PLANTS (I CHOSE KALE.)

## THE STEPS:

**1** | In a well-ventilated area, wear your safety glasses, a mask, and disposable gloves and apply spray paint to the doll bed. Allow to dry.

**2** | Because each doll bed has different dimensions, I will share how I estimated how much chicken wire and coconut coir I would need for mine. Take your chicken wire roll and unroll it so it covers the width of the doll bed (upside down). Unroll the chicken wire a little further so you have excess to work with. Slide the coconut coir layer in between the doll bed and the chicken wire.

**3** | Carefully turn the doll bed, chicken wire, and coconut coir so it is right-side up. You will want to estimate how much of a bend you will need for the wire and coconut coir to accommodate potting soil. Using your hand, gently push down on the coconut coir and chicken wire in the center of the doll bed so that it dips down. You want to allow for these two layers to dip about 4 inches (10 cm) down, but they should not touch the surface you are working on. Bend the chicken wire (still attached to the roll) for where it meets the other side of the doll bed at this time. This is to mark where you will cut the wire free from the roll. Trim the chicken wire free from the roll.

**4** | Turn the doll bed upside down. Place a long edge of the coconut coir on top of the doll bed. Then, place the chicken wire layer on top. Use your staple gun to attach one side of the chicken wire to the bottom bed frame.

4

**5** | Carefully turn the entire project upside down. In the spot where you bent the chicken wire is where you can use the staple gun to attach the chicken wire to the doll bed frame. If you need to trim the coconut coir layer so it fits, you can do so now with scissors. Once the chicken wire is secured, wearing work gloves, use the wire cutters to cut the chicken wire free from the roll. Use your staple gun to attach to the two shorter ends of the wire to the doll bed. At this point, all edges of the chicken wire and doll bed are secured.

**6** | Fold the cut pieces of chicken wire inward. Both cut ends should be twisted so they face each other. Repeat this for all cut edges.

**7** | Turn the bed right-side up. Check that the chicken wire and coconut coir is bowed so that the lowest point is at the center. Add potting soil until the entire "bed" is level with the soil mixture.

**8** | Plant your seedlings or young plants. For my Shady Garden Bed, I planted six dwarf kale plants (two rows, three in each row). Water after planting.

## GROWING KALE FOR BABY GREENS

If you are going to grow leafy greens, you need to try kale (*Brassica oleracea*). There are many strains available for baby greens as well as micro versions to choose from.

Kale likes rich soil that is well draining. When it comes to feeding, I like to use a fertilizer that has a high nitrogen level, which helps promote leafy growth. When growing baby leaves, you can sow new seeds every four to five weeks to ensure a steady supply. If you are growing a dwarf variety to full size, wait until the plant has at least six leaves before you begin to harvest the outer leaves.

I need to protect my kale from the moths that like to use it as a host plant, so I cover my plants in a floating row cover. You can use *Btk* insecticide on the plants as well—it will kill the caterpillars as they eat the plant. (I opt not to because other portions of my garden are designed to attract butterflies for their full life cycle.)

A light frost actually improves kale's flavor by making it sweeter tasting. Kales are rich in antioxidants and in addition to salads, can be used in smoothies or baked as kale chips.

Kale comes in different leaf textures and colors. It can be a delicious design element when used in your micro edible planters.

# COOL COOKIE CONTAINER COMBO

When looking for items that do double duty as containers, take a look in your food pantry. Cookie tins can be repurposed into small containers when you drill holes in the underside for drainage. Compact in size, they fit easily on a kitchen countertop near a sunny window or under grow lights.

When growing indoors, I find that plants that grow well in cool seasons work well for this project. No matter what the temperature is outside, inside with ambient heat or air-conditioning, the plants will acclimate easily (as opposed to warm-season plants that really want to thrive in the heat).

If space is at a premium indoors, this project can be set up outside as a table centerpiece during the cool growing season. You can either start your seeds at the beginning of the cool season or toward the end of the warm season. Some plants can be sown directly and thinned as they grow, while for others it might be easier to transplant them into the cookie tin when they are 2–3 inches tall (5–7.5 cm).

I planted chard, mustard plants, and cabbage in my tin.

## WHAT YOU'LL NEED

- A TIN COOKIE CONTAINER (I USED A ROUND ONE THAT MEASURED 7.5 × 4 × 4 INCHES [19 × 10 × 10 CM].)
- SAFETY GLASSES
- POWER DRILL
- ⁷⁄₆₄-INCH (2.8 MM) DRILL BIT
- PEA GRAVEL
- POTTING SOIL
- PLANTS AND/OR SEEDS

## THE STEPS:

**1** | Take your empty cookie tin and wash it with dish soap and water. Allow to dry.

**2** | Flip the cookie tin upside down. Put on your safety glasses. Using your power drill, drill four evenly spaced holes in the bottom.

**3** | Turn the cookie tin right-side up and add a thin layer of pea gravel to the bottom of the tin. Next, fill with potting soil.

**4** | You can sow seeds directly into your tin and then plan to thin later, or you can transplant in small seedlings. I opted for the seedlings. For my combo, I visually divided the container into thirds and planted swiss chard, cabbage, and mustard plant seedlings. After planting, water with a sprinkler-head attachment.

## WHAT'S THE DEAL ON MUSTARDS?

Mustard plants (*Brassica juncea*) can be sown every three weeks for a continual harvest. Mustard plants range in size, but they make a wonderful addition to salads when grown as a baby leaf variety, and they add spice and color to stir-fry meals. The greens are often used in Asian and African meals and are popular in the southern United States. For plants started during the warm season, a light frost as the weather begins to cool can improve the flavor of the plant. Leaves are ready to be harvested when the reach 6 to 8 inches (15 to 20.5 cm) tall.

## TIPS FOR GROWING
## PETITE CABBAGES

Dwarf varieties of cabbage (*Brassica oleracea*) do best in cool weather in full sun. They can be grown in a container as long as you provide consistent moisture. Infrequent watering or heat can stress the plant, which can be a reason it does not form a cabbage head.

## PLANT CHOICES

● ● ●

Looking for ideas for what you can grow in your cookie tin? Below are some suggestions. Seedlings purchased from garden shops or plants you started from seed ahead of time are referred to as "transplant" below. (The seedling should have developed at least two or three sets of true leaves.)

| PLANT | RECOMMENDATION |
| --- | --- |
| MINI CABBAGE<br>(*Brassica oleracea*) | Transplant |
| KALE (baby greens)<br>(*Brassica napus*) | Direct sow or transplant |
| BOK CHOY<br>(*Brassica rapa*) | Transplant |
| MUSTARD (baby greens)<br>(*Brassica juncea*) | Direct sow or transplant |
| CHARD<br>(*Beta vulgaris*) | Direct sow or transplant |

# OMELET COMBO

> **THIS PROJECT CAN BE GROWN INDOORS.**

If you have not already guessed, I love to grow micro edibles to use as garnishes for meals. Sometimes, I just need a little bit, so instead of devoting a large container to one crop, I thought, what if I just had a little bit of what I needed available on my countertop? Using a wooden caddy and mason jars, I was able to grow six ingredients that could be snipped and added to my omelet recipe, without using up the entire plant.

## WHAT YOU'LL NEED

- (6) 32-OUNCE (946 ML) WIDE-MOUTH MASON JARS
- SAFETY GLASSES
- TOWEL
- POWER DRILL
- ½-INCH (12.7 MM) DIAMOND DRILL BIT
- COOL WATER
- PEA GRAVEL
- POTTING SOIL
- SEEDS
- PLASTIC WRAP
- WOODEN TOOL CADDY

## THE STEPS:

**1** | For each mason jar, you'll need to use your diamond bit to drill a hole in the bottom for drainage. Center your drill bit on the glass as much as possible—this helps ensure a clean drill hole without shattering the glass jar. If you drill a hole closer to the side of the jar, you have a better chance of cracking the glass. With the jar upside down on the towel and wearing your safety glasses, hold your drill so the drill bit is touching the glass at a 45-degree angle. Use a slow speed and as you drill, you'll need to add water periodically so that the glass does not overheat. If the glass overheats, it can break.

**2** | As the drill bit starts to scratch the glass, you can gradually move your arm so that your drill is eventually at a 90-degree angle. You'll want to keep the drill on a low to medium speed and continue to add water occasionally as you drill. The real trick for this is to be patient. It takes me about 10–15 minutes to drill a hole into the glass mason jar. If you find yourself becoming impatient or trying to increase the drill speed, the best bet is to take a quick break. (But just think of the upper arm strength you will have after drilling six mason jars!)

**3** | You'll know that you are close to cutting through the glass completely when the pitch of the grinding noise changes. Throughout the drilling process, the drill bit sounds about the same, but the drilling will increase in pitch right before you succeed in cutting the hole. Be sure to not be pushing down into the glass jar at this point, because if you are pushing down into the glass with your drill, once the hole is cut, the impact of the drill coming down hard on the mason jar can break it. (It's so disappointing to break the mason jar at this stage—so do your best not to get distracted or let your mind wander.) Clean up the glass shards that have collected on the towel from drilling the hole.

**4** | Turn your mason jar right-side up and fill it with about ½ inch (1.5 cm) of pea gravel. Then, fill the jar with potting soil so that only the top ¼ remains empty. Now is the time to sow your seeds. Follow the seed packet instructions for the amount of soil you place on top. You'll want to scatter about 5–10 seeds into your mason jar, depending on how large the seeds are. After the seeds are sown, water with a sprinkler attachment. I then place a small piece of plastic wrap on the mouth of the jar to create a mini greenhouse inside and encourage germination. Place the mason jar under your grow light or in a sunny windowsill. For easy storage and mobility, I placed all six finished mason jars in a wooden tool caddy.

## 5

## TIPS ON STARTING PARSLEY SEEDS

• • •

Parsley (*Petroselinum crispum*) takes a while to germinate, so don't get discouraged if it takes a week or two for the seedlings to poke through the soil's surface. Before sowing, soak your seeds in lukewarm water for up to 24 hours. This will help with germination.

Parsley is a biennial plant, meaning that it will flower in its second year—but you grow it for the leaves. When harvesting your parsley, use sharp scissors to snip the outer stems first, leaving the newer stems to grow closer to the center.

**5** | Once the seeds sprout, remove the plastic wrap and continue to water when the soil looks dry. As the seedlings grow, you'll need to thin the plants so no more than 3 remain in the jar.

Choose the largest and healthiest of the seeds and either use scissors to trim the extras at the soil line or gently tug them out and remove. After thinning, water your seedlings to resettle the soil in the jar. (This is an especially good practice after pulling the plants out in order to remove any air pockets that might form in the disturbed soil.)

**6** | When the plants reach about 4–5 inches (10–13 cm) high, you will be able to start harvesting them for use in your meals.

## WHAT TO GROW IN YOUR MASON JARS
## AND HOW TO HARVEST

• • •

| WHAT TO GROW | WHEN TO HARVEST | HOW TO HARVEST |
| --- | --- | --- |
| BABY SPINACH (*Spinacia oleracea*) | When leaves are at least 2 inches (5 cm) long. | Harvest leaves from the outside in. |
| CHIVES (*Allium schoenoprasum*) | When the plant is at least 6 inches (15 cm) tall. | Snip leaves from the outside in and leave at least 2 inches (5 cm) of the plant (do not cut down to the ground). |
| CHARD (*Beta vulgaris*) | When the plant is at least 6 inches (15 cm) tall. | Cut individual leaves. |
| FERNLEAF DILL (*Anethum graveolens*) | Foliage can be snipped when the plant has at least 4 to 5 leaves. | Pinch or snip older leaves first. |
| PARSLEY (*Petroselinum crispum*) | Stems need at least three clusters of leaves before they can be harvested. | Cut at the base of the plant, harvesting from the outside in. |
| BABY KALE (*Brassica oleracea*) | When leaves are about 4 inches (10 cm) tall. | Snip stems, leaving about 2 inches (5 cm) on the plant so it can regrow. |
| BABY ARUGULA (*Eruca sativa*) | When leaves are between 2 and 3 inches long (5 to 7.5 cm). | Harvest leaves from the outside in. |

# SPROUTS

▶ THIS PROJECT CAN BE
GROWN INDOORS.

Growing sprouts reminds me a bit like tending to sourdough starter. They both need attention—up to two times a day for maintenance—but both have the ability to you look pretty great when they are ready to use. For a long time, I didn't grow sprouts because I thought it would be hard to do.

It's actually really easy.

There are lots of seeds that can be used for sprouts, which pack lots of nutrients and flavor in each bite. In this way, they are similar to micro-greens (page 152). But they are different than microgreens because sprouts are able to grow without soil. They are grown in a container that is initially soaked to begin the process and then rinsed and spun twice a day until they are ready to be consumed.

You can eat fresh sprouts (raw) or you can cook them and add them to meals. Raw sprouts do carry a risk of food-borne illness, so in the United States, the Centers for Disease Control and Prevention (CDC) recommends thoroughly cooking sprouts before consuming in order to avoid food poisoning risks. According to the University of California Division of Agriculture and Natural Resources, "People in high-risk categories such as children, pregnant women, the elderly, and people with weakened

## WHAT YOU'LL NEED

- CLEANED AND SANITIZED SPROUTING CONTAINERS
- SPROUTING SEEDS FROM A REPUTABLE COMPANY
- TABLESPOON
- WATER

immune systems are advised not to eat raw sprouts." Cooked sprouts can be eaten when heated to above 165°F (74°C).

This sounds serious, but mainly drives home the importance of growing sprouts correctly. Kitchen sanitation plays a role here, too. The container you will use needs to be washed with dish soap and water and dried before using. **You should only use seeds from reputable companies. These packets are marked for "sprouting" purposes and are certified as "pathogen-free" seeds.** (This is to reduce the risk of illness from seeds that are either treated or not cleaned for eating raw sprouts.) Reputable seed houses even send out a portion of their seeds to get tested to verify that the batches are clean from food-borne diseases.

There are a variety of ways you can sprout seeds, including purchasing a special sprouting container to streamline the process or by purchasing a sprout jar lid, which can be used with a wide-mouth mason jar.

This project requires you to check in on it daily, so it is not a project where you start seeds and return a few days later.

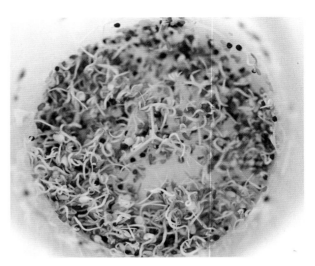

Sprouts are a great way to grow a micro edible quickly on a kitchen countertop. You should only use seeds marked for sprouting and sold from reputable companies to aid food safety.

## THE STEPS:

**1** | On day 1, measure out a half tablespoon (enough for about three to four meals) or a tablespoon (enough for four to six meals) of your sprouting seeds. Follow the seed-prep guidelines. (See the project sidebar on page 146.)

**2** | Rinse the seeds under water. Add the seeds to your sprouting container for soaking. Fill with 1 cup (235 ml) of lukewarm water and let the seeds soak for eight hours.

**3** | Drain the water the seeds were soaking in and rinse your seeds under running water. You will want to get the excess water out of the container. I use a sprouting container, so I spin my seeds over the sink, which uses centrifugal motion to get the excess water out. (Check your sprouting container for the recommended way.) Once the water has been spun out, let the sprouts sit for another 12 hours.

**4** | For days 2–5, you will do the following twice a day (every 12 hours): Rinse and spin the seeds and then let them sit on the counter until it is time to rinse and spin again. (You can set a timer to remind you.) It is important to follow this schedule to prevent bacterial growth on the sprouts. If you see mold on your sprouts, that means there was too much moisture in your container. Discard the seeds and begin again with a new batch.

**5** | As the sprouts grow, they will begin to fill the container as they expand vertically. Once the sprouts are roughly 2 inches (5 cm) in length, you can add them to your meals. (You can also eat them when they are under 2 inches [5 cm].) Give them a final rinse and spin. You want to be good about rinsing and draining the seeds because excess moisture can shorten the storage life. You can skim and remove the hulls—the outer coating of the seed—from your sprouts. (Hulls can also make the sprouts spoil faster, and removing them generally improves the flavor.) You can also store them in a refrigerator (for up to three days).

## SAFE SPROUTING TIPS

To minimize the chances of food-borne illness, it is important to disinfect the outside of your seeds and your container before sprouting. Here are the steps:

- Sanitize your sprouting container by following the directions on the bleach container for sanitizing kitchen surfaces. Use plain bleach—not scented laundry bleach. Use ¾ cup (175 ml) of bleach per gallon (3.8 L) of water (3 tablespoons [45 ml] per quart [946 ml]) and soak the container for at least 5 minutes. Then, rinse with clean water.

- Using a small pot, heat 3% hydrogen peroxide until it reaches 140°F (60°C). Use a clean digital cooking thermometer during this process. When the solution has reached the temperature, take your measured amount of seeds and place it in a small mesh strainer and immerse it into the heated solution. You will heat this on the stovetop for five minutes. Swirl the strainer at one-minute intervals to ensure the seeds are coated.

- Rinse the seeds in running tap water for 1 minute. Next, put the rinsed seeds in a container with enough tap water to reach about 1 inch (2.5 cm) above the seeds.

- Skim off the floating seed and seed coat fragments. These can be discarded into the trash.

- If you are doing more than one batch of sprouting seeds, replace your hydrogen peroxide solution in between uses.

- Move the seeds to your clean, sanitized container for sprouting. This container should be away from areas of food prep, pests, and high household traffic.

*Source: University of California Division of Agriculture and Natural Resources (See the Resources section for more information.)*

## TYPES OF SPROUTS

• • •

You can purchase a single variety or a combination of sprouting mixes to grow. Always use seed from reputable seed companies that test their batches for *E. coli* 0157 and salmonella. The seed packets should also be labeled for sprouting purposes. Here are some common seeds used for sprouting:

| SEED TYPE | FLAVOR/TRAIT | READY TO HARVEST |
|---|---|---|
| ALFALFA (*Medicago sativa*) | Nutty | 4–6 days |
| RED CLOVER (*Trifolium pratense*) | Mild | 5–7 days |
| BROCCOLI (*Brassica oleracea* var. *italica*) | Spicy | 5–9 days |
| KALE (*Brassica napus*) | Mild | 5–7 days |
| MUSTARD (*Brassica juncea*) | Hot and spicy | 4–5 days |
| MUNG BEAN (*Vigna radiata*) | Similar to garden peas | 4–6 days |
| PURPLE KOHLRABI (*Brassica oleracea* var. *gongylodes*) | Brassica flavor with spicy notes | 6–8 days |

# CREATE YOUR OWN INDOOR GROW LIGHT

▶ THIS PROJECT IS FOR USE INDOORS.

If lighting can be considered a garden tool, then my grow light fixtures are ones I rely on heavily. They make a huge difference when you live in a space that is on the darker side and allow you to get a jump start on the growing season by providing a strong and steady light source indoors. I like to start my micro edible varieties by seed, so that way I can grow what I want without relying on finding the plants in spring at the retail stores.

When using grow lights to start seeds, I plug mine into an automatic timer so that the plants receive continuous light each day, without relying on me to turn the light fixture on and off. I have my grow light on for 14 hours of light a day.

There are several different types of grow lights available, and sometimes the choices can be overwhelming. Over time, I have switched over to LED bulbs—they use less energy and do not get as hot as the fluorescent models.

## WHAT YOU'LL NEED

- 2-FOOT (61 CM) LED LIGHT FIXTURE WITH HANGING WIRES AND LIGHT SHIELD
- (4) ¾-INCH × 2-FOOT (2 × 61 CM) PVC PIPES
- (2) ¾- × ¾-INCH (2 × 2 CM)-DIAMETER SLIP ELBOW PVC FITTINGS
- (2) ¾- × ¾-INCH (2 × 2 CM)-DIAMETER TEE PVC FITTINGS
- (4) ¾-INCH (2 CM) PVC END CAPS
- TAPE MEASURE
- MARKER
- WORK GLOVES
- SAFETY GLASSES
- PVC PIPE CUTTER (ABLE TO CUT ¾-INCH [2 CM] PIPES)
- CLEAR, HEAVY-DUTY GLUE
- DISPOSABLE GLOVES

When looking for a grow light fixture, I opt for full-spectrum lights. Grow lights can be labeled by color spectrum: Red light encourages plants to produce flowers and fruit, while blue light encourages foliage and roots. Full spectrum lights provide a balance of both, so you don't need to worry about buying the correct combination.

When shopping for a fixture, you'll want one that is UL or ETL listed, which ensures that the fixture is safe for use in your home. Grow light fixtures can also be lightweight, which is the style I used for this project.

This grow light project is designed to fit on top of a table, dresser, or cabinet in your home, being less than 15 inches (38 cm) wide. It's perfect for microgreens (page 152) or extra light for your Omelet Combo (page 138).

## THE STEPS:

**1** | Take two of the 2-foot (61 cm) PVC pipes and attach a slip elbow fitting to one end and a tee PVC fitting to the other end.

**2** | Attach a 2-foot (61 cm) PVC pipe to each of the slip elbow fittings, connecting all three pieces.

**3** | Take the two remaining PVC pipes and use the tape measure to mark four 6-inch (15 cm) segments. Wearing your safety glasses and work gloves, cut the pipe where the marks are with your pipe cutter, so you are left with four pieces.

**4** | Attach each 6-inch (15 cm) piece to the tee PVC fitting, so that the structure now has legs. Attach the end caps to the remaining open sides of the PVC pipes.

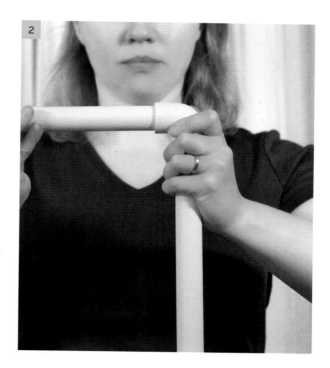

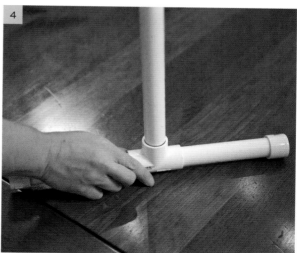

5 | Wearing disposable gloves, add a thin layer of glue to where the PVC pipes meet the elbow and tee fittings. This has to be done outside or in a spot with good airflow. Allow to dry. This will help ensure that the grow light fixture stays together and does not loosen and come apart.

6 | Use the hanging wires included with your grow light to suspend the grow light from the top. Adjust the grow light to the plant you have beneath it. (See the project sidebar for recommended heights.)

## HEIGHTS FOR THE LIGHTS

When you first set up your grow light, you will want it to sit above the seedlings you have planted, leaving approximately a 4-inch (10 cm) gap. As the seeds sprout and grow, you will move that grow light fixture up, so that way, the plants never have a chance to touch the bulb. It's also important to move the light upward so the seedlings do not get burned.

You do not want to start with the light suspended too high because then the seedlings will get "leggy" and will stretch toward the light.

More mature plants can have the grow light suspended 12–30 inches (30.5–76 cm) from the top of the plant.

## HOW TO MAKE A
## TWO-TIER GROW LIGHT AREA

If you have a narrow footprint free, you can consider adding a grow light shelf system, which will not only double your available space but also the amount of seeds you can grow. You can find a metal shelving unit online or at hardware stores or discount stores. You will want to pick out the grow light you want to use first and make sure your metal shelving unit is slightly longer and wider than the light. You can use plastic zip ties to attach your grow light to the underside of the shelf, or if your grow light includes hooks, you can use them for hanging, too.

When using a metal shelving unit to grow seeds, you will want to include a plastic tray to place your seed starting containers inside. This way, when you water your seedling, the extra water that drains out will not spill onto your floor. If you use an automatic timer with your grow lights, they will turn on and off automatically to the programmed time.

You can double your growing area by thinking vertically. Use a metal shelving system to hang two compact grow light fixtures.

# MICROGREENS

Guess what? If you have grown any edible from seed, you already have some knowledge on how to grow microgreens.

Of course, when growing said plants from seed, you most likely continue to nurture it past its infant stage. Microgreens, on the other hand, are edible plants only grown for their first set of leaves because of the available nutrients they offer. This means that microgreens are a great way to add nutrition to your sandwiches and salads.

They are different from growing sprouts (see page 143) because microgreens are grown in soil in shallow trays, while sprouts are grown using a system of soaking and rinsing the seeds—without any soil.

Microgreens can be grown in a sunny windowsill or under a grow light (see page 148 on how to make your own). When choosing your indoor growing area, keep in mind the ideal growing temperature to sprout microgreens is between 65–75°F (18.3–24°C). You can continue to sow microgreens every 14 days to have a continuous supply—and the best part is that this can be done all year round!

## WHAT YOU'LL NEED

- DISPOSABLE PIE PAN
- FORK
- SEED STARTING SOIL MIXTURE
- VERMICULITE (OPTIONAL)
- MICROGREEN SEEDS

For this project, I used a disposable pie pan to grow my microgreen seeds in (with a tray underneath to collect excess water). You can get two to three uses out of each pie plate—just remove the soil and roots from harvested microgreens (great food for your worm bin!) and wash with dish soap and allow to dry before replanting.

## THE STEPS:

**1** | Use the fork to puncture drainage holes in the disposable pie pan.

**2** | Add your soil to the pie dish, leaving about ½ inch (1.5 cm) from the top.

**3** | Sow your microgreen seeds. You can be generous in your sowing.

**4** | Top your seeds with soil or vermiculite so it reaches the inside lip of the pie plate. Skip this step if your seed packet recommends that you scatter the seeds on top of the soil but do not cover.

**5** | Water your seeds with a sprinkler head watering can or a plant mister.

**6** | Set your pie plate under your light source.

### GROWING TIP

You can use a humidity dome to place over the pie plate, similar to what you would do to trap moisture for seed starting. This will speed up germination, but is not necessary.

## HOW TO HARVEST MICROGREENS

When seedlings emerge, the first two leaves are called cotyledons. These two leaves will look different than the future leaves of the plant, called the "true leaves." When comparing microgreen seeds, you'll notice that appearance of the first set of true leaves is a way to determine when the microgreen is ready to harvest. Microgreens vary in growing time—some are faster or slower and can vary between 10 to 25 days. They will vary on height—usually between ½ to 2 inches (1.5 to 5 cm)—which will include the cotyledons and at least one pair of true leaves.

You can use a clean pair of scissors to harvest your microgreens. Cut at the soil line and then rinse under running water before using.

Microgreens are best used right after harvesting for their peak nutritional value, but they can be stored in a refrigerator in a sealed container for five days if needed.

## WHAT CAN YOU USE MICROGREENS FOR?

I like to add microgreens on top of hamburgers. You can add them as toppings for salads, sandwiches, and wraps, too. Microgreens can also add flavor to stir-fry dishes, omelets, and sushi.

# A QUICK LOOK AT MICROGREENS

Microgreen seeds can be exclusive to one variety or available as mixtures that have common characteristics, such as spicy or mild.

| SEED TYPE | FLAVOR/TRAIT | READY TO HARVEST |
| --- | --- | --- |
| ARUGULA (*Eruca sativa*) | Spicy, nutty | 10–15 days |
| AMARANTH (*Amaranthus cruentus*) | Mild, earthy | 16–25 days |
| BASIL (*Ocimum basilicum*) | Sweet to spicy | 16–25 days |
| BEETS (*Beta vulgaris*) | Earthy | 16–25 days |
| BROCCOLI (*Brassica oleracea*) | Mild | 10–15 days |
| CHARD (*Beta vulgaris*) | Earthy | 16–25 days |
| KALE (*Brassica oleracea*) | Mild | 10–15 days |
| KOHLRABI (*Brassiaca oleracea*) | Mild | 10–15 days |
| MUSTARD (*Brassica juncea*) | Spicy | 10–15 days |
| RADISH (*Raphanus sativus*) | Spicy | 10–15 days |

# MUFFIN PAN BASIL

When I'm making meals, I like to have access to fresh herbs, but without giving up the limited real estate on my kitchen counter. That's how I started to grow mini basil plants (*Ocimum basilicum*). Officially known as a microgreen, they pack the same flavorful punch as full-sized basil plants. Mini basil seedlings make a delicious addition to appetizers, sandwiches, salads, and more.

Growing basil microgreens in a muffin pan provides quick access to the herb. You can set a tray under a tabletop grow light (see page 148) or in a sunny windowsill. (For more types of micro-greens you can grow, see page 152.) While most small-space gardeners only have room for one or two full-sized basil plants, micro food garden-ers can grow a continuous harvest of mini basil microgreens for flavor that's available all year.

## WHAT YOU'LL NEED

- DISPOSABLE ALUMINUM 6-CUP MUFFIN PAN
- A FORK
- POTTING SOIL

- BASIL SEEDS (SEE THE CHART ON PAGE 159 FOR SUGGESTIONS.)
- 1-GALLON (3.8 L) (OR LARGER) PLASTIC FOOD-GRADE BAG

When grown as mini plants, you can grow different types of basil to discover all the different flavor possibilities. One variety that does well in a disposable muffin pan is Greek basil. It is compact, produces mini leaves, and grows in a dome shape. You can experiment with larger size varieties as well, allowing them to grow 2–3 inches (5–7.5 cm) tall before harvesting them.

## THE STEPS:

**1** | Start by using your fork to puncture holes in the muffin pan. Holding the pan in one hand, use the fork to gently push the prongs through the bottom of the muffin cup. Do this once per muffin cup, so when you are finished, you will have four holes in each muffin cup.

**2** | Fill the muffin cups with dampened potting soil so the soil is level with the top of the tray.

**3** | Sprinkle your basil seeds on top of the potting soil. Lightly press the seeds down into the soil. Cover lightly with potting soil. Water gently with a mister.

4

**4** | Place the muffin pan into the plastic bag and seal it. This will create a little greenhouse to help the basil seeds sprout. Once the basil sprouts (approximately 5 to 10 days), take the muffin pan out of the plastic bag and place it under your grow light or in the sunny spot to continue growing. You can place a second muffin tray underneath to catch any excess water. Keep the soil moist as the little plants grow.

**5** | Start harvesting your basil after it develops its second set of leaves (called the "true" leaves) by pinching the stems off right above the soil line or snipping them off with a pair of scissors. Microgreens will not regrow from the roots. See the project sidebar for tips on extending the harvest.

## CONTINUING THE HARVEST

If you'd like to provide a steady harvest of mini basil babies, here are a few methods to try:

1. Plant all 6 muffin tin cups at the same time for a bigger one-time harvest or fill and plant one cup every week to extend the harvest. Then, when a cup has been fully harvested, replant it again to keep the cycle going.

2. Start a whole new muffin pan with seeds every other week so you constantly have more growing.

3. Allow the plants to grow out of the microgreen stage and develop two or three sets of "true" leaves. Harvest the tips of these slightly more mature plants by pinching off only the top set of leaves while leaving the lower sets intact. Harvesting this way allows the plants to resprout for multiple harvests from the same plant.

## WHAT TYPE OF SEEDS
## SHOULD YOU GROW?

• • •

There are many types of basil (*Ocimum basilicum*) that can be used for this project. Here are some of my favorites.

| VARIETY | TASTE |
|---------|-------|
| GREEK BASIL (*Ocimum minimum*) | Spicy, anise flavor |
| LEMON BASIL (*Ocimum americanum*) | Lemon fragrance and flavor |
| LETTUCE LEAF BASIL (*Ocimum basilicum* 'Lettuce Leaf') | Sweet |
| THAI BASIL (*Ocimum basilicum* var. *thyrsiflorum*) | Licorice flavor |
| GENOVESE BASIL (*Ocimum basilicum* 'Genovese Gigante') | Classic basil used for pesto |

# WINDOWSILL PEA SHOOTS

> **THIS PROJECT CAN BE GROWN INDOORS.**

Growing pea shoots (*Pisum sativum*) in mason jars is a great way to maximize your growing space on your window ledge. I like to grow mine on the window ledge above my kitchen sink. As the pea shoots grow, you can snip them with scissors and add to your salads or stir-fry meals. You'll get about three rounds of cuttings before needing to switch to a new set of seeds. If you are using a lot of pea shoots in your meals, you can sow pea seeds every five to seven days to provide a continuous supply.

Of course, I like to add drainage holes to my mason jars, so when I water, the extra liquid can drain quickly. You can opt to skip this step (and I give the directions for how to drill into glass jars to the right), but you will need to keep an eye on the water level that collects at the bottom of the jar.

## WHAT YOU'LL NEED

- 16-OUNCE (475 ML) WIDE-MOUTH MASON JAR
- SMALL STONES, SUCH AS PEA GRAVEL
- POTTING SOIL
- PEA SEEDS

**IF NOT DRILLING DRAINAGE HOLES:**

- CHARCOAL

**IF DRILLING A DRAINAGE HOLE:**

- SAFETY GLASSES
- POWER DRILL
- ½-INCH (12.7 MM) DIAMOND DRILL BIT
- TOWEL
- TAPE (MASKING OR BLUE PAINTER'S TAPE)
- WATERING CAN WITH COLD WATER

# THE STEPS:

## TO DRILL DRAINAGE HOLES INTO MASON JARS:

**1** | Put on your safety glasses. Lay your towel on the table and place the mason jar on top, upside down. Place a small piece of masking or painter's tape at the bottom where you want to drill your hole for drainage.

**2** | Position your drill at a 45-degree angle and on a slow speed, begin to mark the tape on the glass. You'll only want to scratch the glass at this point in order to give the drill bit something to catch as you continue to drill.

**3** | Once your glass is scratched, remove the tape. On the lowest setting for your hand drill, position your drill at a 45-degree angle and continue to drill. Stop periodically as you drill to add cold water to the spot where you are drilling the hole. This is to prevent the glass from over-heating and cracking.

**4** | As you continue to (slowly) drill, move your hand so you gradually move from 45-degree angle to a 90-degree angle. Continue to stop and add water to the surface as needed and drill at slow speed. Do not push into the mason jar as you drill. The extra force could crack it when the drill makes the final cut for the hole.

**5** | Once the hole is created in the glass, carefully remove your drill bit from the hole by reversing the direction of the drill bit and slowly running it until it is removed. Use a piece of tape to remove any loose shards of glass from the hole.

### STEPS FOR PLANTING THE PEA SEEDS:

**1** | Fill your mason jar with a thin layer of small stones (about ½ inch [1.5 cm]).

**2** | If you are working with mason jars that do not have a drainage hole, add a ½-inch (1.5 cm) layer of charcoal on top of the stones. This extra layer of drainage helps in preventing root rot. (If your mason jar has drainage, you can skip this step.)

**3** | Add your potting soil to the jar, leaving about 2 inches (5 cm) free from the top. Sow your pea seeds.

## HOW TO HARVEST YOUR PEA SHOOTS

For one-time use, when the pea shoots have reached between 3 and 4 inches (7.5–10 cm) tall, you can harvest them by cutting them at the soil line.

For multiple harvests (up to three), leave about ½ inch (1.5 cm) of growth (above the first two leaves, or cotyledons) so the plant can regrow.

# CONCLUSION

◇◆◇◆◇◆◇

Growing your own food is a practice that is here to stay—and it is possible for plants to prosper in the smallest of spaces.

I hope these projects spur your imagination and inspire you to create your own unique micro edible projects. When searching for micro edibles, read seed packets and plant tags to find plants that will grow 18 inches (46 cm) or smaller. Consider plant varieties that are labeled as "container friendly." Provide them with the light, water, and soil nutrients they need to thrive—at the same time, you will nurture your green thumb.

I encourage you to be adventurous! When writing this book, I also came across plants that I had heard about but had not grown previously, such as bok choy and watercress. I was happy to find that they were easy to cultivate. They will remain in my garden in the future.

When deciding what type of projects I wanted to create, I searched for miniature varieties of plants and was happy to find so many options to choose from. When you grow micro food projects, you may find yourself looking at the items in your life in a different way. Suddenly, the challenge of transforming an everyday object into a container for growing micro edibles can lead to some interesting creations. Coming up with the projects for this book was exciting and fun as I tested the limits to see what was possible. And boy, do those micro food plants perform!

Be creative in what you choose for containers. What can be repurposed to fit in a small area of your home, patio, or entrance way? Find plants that will flourish in the space you have, and if you are inspired, add grow lights to darker portions of your home to expand your edible repertoire.

Miniature tomatoes come in all shapes and sizes.

Consider the ways you can improve the lifespan of your project, such as adding proper drainage holes and installing plastic liners to prevent warping in materials that retain moisture (such as wood).

But not all projects need to be in coffee cups or cookie tins. Many micro edibles can be grown in smaller garden containers and window boxes you can find at your independent garden center or online.

Understanding what a plant needs to grow to its fullest potential is important. If you have deep shade, a fruiting plant like a tomato will not be able to live its best life in that spot because it will be constantly seeking more sun.

◀ Even the tiniest edible plant can yield food, such as these micro pea plants.

Blossoms on a dwarf watermelon plant are ready for pollination.

Throughout this book, I've shared examples of plants that can be used in the projects. As you grow with the plants, you'll start noticing the conditions that they prefer. Soon, you will find that other plants share similar growing requirements. As this happens, you'll be able to look at this book in a new light. This book was first designed as a primer to introduce you to the world of micro edibles. As you become more familiar with the plants and their growing habits, you may view some of the projects differently. For example, maybe you will want to grow miniature peas in coffee cans and bush beans in the bicycle basket. Feel free to experiment and swap plants that share similar characteristics for the projects in the book.

No matter which project you choose, remember to check on your plant daily, especially during hot temperatures. You'll be more successful in growing your micro food if you make the plant care part of your routine.

Also, aim for ways you can use your project containers again when the crop has finished. This is especially true for fast-growing crops, like lettuce. The more you plant, the more comfortable and knowledgeable you will become.

I am confident that you will find a project in this book that will align with your gardening journey—whether you are just starting out and feel more comfortable purchasing plants and transplanting them into containers, or if you are a seed-starting pro and are looking to add something different to the table. If you want to grow something, you can!

▶ Micro food, such as these cabbages, can be grown in a window box.

# RESOURCES

I used the following resources to verify information and have provided them if you are interested in reading more about them.

Badgett, Becca. (2019, June 20). *Eggplant Harvest: Information on How to Harvest An Eggplant*. Gardening Know How. https://www.gardeningknowhow.com/edible/vegetables/eggplant/how-to-harvest-eggplants.htm

Barth, Brain. (2018, March 2). *Grow Lights for Indoor Plants and Indoor Gardening: An Overview*. Modern Farmer. https://modernfarmer.com/2018/03/grow-lights-for-indoor-plants-and-indoor-gardening/

Botanical Interests. *Microgreens and Baby Greens: Sow and Grow Guide*. https://www.botanicalinterests.com/product/Microgreens-and-Baby-Greens-Sow-and-Grow-Guide

Botanical Interests. *Sprouting Seeds at Home: Disinfecting, Growing, and Harvesting Tips*. https://www.botanicalinterests.com/product/Sprouting-Seeds-at-Home-Disinfecting-Growing-and-Harvesting-Tips

Botanical Interests. *Sprouts: Growing Guide*. https://www.botanicalinterests.com/product/Sprouts-Growing-Guide

Dyer, Mary H. (2020, June 29). *Container Grown Cantaloupe: Care of Cantaloupe in Pots*. Gardening Know How. https://www.gardeningknowhow.com/edible/fruits/cantaloupe/care-of-cantaloupe-in-pots.htm

Fisher, Stacy. (2020, June 3). *How to Macramé: 7 Basic Knots to Master*. The Spruce Crafts. https://www.thesprucecrafts.com/basic-macrame-knots-4176636

Johnny's Select Seeds. (2019, December 3). *Microgreens Comparison Chart*. https://www.johnnyseeds.com/growers-library/vegetables/micro-greens-comparison-chart.html

Kellogg, Kristi & Sung, Esther. (2018, September 25). *20 Types of Peppers and Their Uses*. Epicurious. https://www.epicurious.com/ingredients/20-types-of-peppers-and-their-uses-article

Kurtz, Lauren. How to Harvest Parsley. (2020, July 6). In WikiHow. https://www.wikihow.com/Harvest-Parsley

Langellotto, G.A. & Gupta, Abha. (2012). Gardening Increases Vegetable Consumption in School-aged Children: A Meta-analytical Synthesis. *HortTechnology, 22* (4), 430–445. doi: https://doi.org/10.21273/HORTTECH.22.4.430

Lifetime Daily, Contributor. (2017, July 26). *Cucumbers Are Nature's Most Hydrating Vegetable*. Huffpost. https://www.huffingtonpost.ca/lifetime-daily/cucumber-is-nature-s-most-hydrating-vegetable_a_23047972/

McGuinness, Jen. (2018, February 5). Salinas showcases cool-weather crops for home gardener. Frau Zinnie. https://frauzinnie.blogspot.com/2018/02/salinas-showcases-cool-weather-crops.html

Michaels, Kerry. (2020, July 10). *7 Materials Used for Plant Containers*. The Spruce. https://www.thespruce.com/all-about-choosing-plant-containers-847998

Miller, Renee. (2018, December 15). *Vermiculite Vs. Perlite*. SFGate/San Francisco Chronicle. https://homeguides.sfgate.com/vermiculite-vs-perlite-49660.html

Rhoades, Heather. (2020, May 15). *Tips for Growing Cilantro*. Gardening Know How. https://www.gardeningknowhow.com/edible/herbs/cilantro/tips-for-growing-cilantro.htm

Rushing, Felder. *Growing Fingerling Potatoes*. DIY Network. https://www.diynetwork.com/how-to/outdoors/gardening/growing-fingerling-potatoes

Shinn, Meghann. (2018, Dec. 8). *Removing White Crust from Clay Pots*. Horticulture. https://www.hortmag.com/headline/removing-white-crust-from-clay-pots

stylnpzzalvr. *The Best Rain Barrel for Less Than $15, and Where to Find a Barrel*. https://www.instructables.com/id/How-to-make-a-rain-barrel-1/

The Old Farmer's Almanac. *Squash Bugs: How to Identify and Get Rid of Squash Bugs*. https://www.almanac.com/pest/squash-bugs

Thompson & Morgan. (2020). *Edible Flowers Guide*. https://www.thompson-morgan.com/edible-flowers

Tilley, Nikki. (2020, June 8). *Fertilizer Numbers – What Is NPK*. Gardening Know How. https://www.gardeningknowhow.com/garden-how-to/soil-fertilizers/fertilizer-numbers-npk.htm

Uncle Jim's Worm Farm. *FAQs*. https://unclejimswormfarm.com/faqs/

United States Environmental Protection Agency. *How to Create and Maintain an Indoor Worm Composting Bin*. https://www.epa.gov/recycle/how-create-and-maintain-indoor-worm-composting-bin

University of Arizona, College of Agriculture & Life Sciences. *Tatsoi*. https://cals.arizona.edu/fps/sites/cals.arizona.edu.fps/files/cotw/Tatsoi.pdf

University of California, Division of Agriculture and Natural Resources. (2004). *Growing Seed Sprouts at Home*. Publication 8151. https://anrcatalog.ucanr.edu/pdf/8151.pdf

University of California, Agriculture and Natural Resources. *About Worm Castings*. https://ucanr.edu/sites/mgfresno/files/262372.pdf

University of Florida Institute of Food and Agricultural Sciences. (2016, September 19). *Gardening as a child may lead college students to eat more veggies*. ScienceDaily. www.sciencedaily.com/releases/2016/09/160919110301.htm

Vanderlinden, Colleen. (2019, November 3). *Make a Worm-Composting Bin from Plastic Buckets*. The Spruce. https://www.thespruce.com/inexpensive-worm-bin-from-plastic-buckets-2540077

Walliser, Jessica. *Common Cucumber Plant Problems*. Savvy Gardening. https://savvygardening.com/cucumber-plant-problems/

Ware, Megan. (2019, November 4). *What to know about watercress*. Medical News Today: Diet. https://www.medicalnewstoday.com/articles/285412#diet

Watercress. (2020, August 22). In *Wikipedia*. https://en.wikipedia.org/wiki/Watercress

World Economic Forum. (2020). *Global Future Council on Cities and Urbanization*. https://www.weforum.org/communities/the-future-of-cities-and-urbanization

The following seed companies for information on how to grow specific plants (seed packets and websites): Botanical Interests; Burpee; High Mowing Seeds; Johnny's Select Seeds; Renee's Garden Seeds; Sandia Seed.

# MEET JEN MCGUINNESS

**Jen McGuinness** is a writer, editor, photographer, and a life-long gardener. She is a proponent of growing your own food using organic and pollinator-friendly methods. Her photos have been published in magazines and newspapers, and she is an award-winning former journalist. She has been blogging as Frau Zinnie (FrauZinnie.com) since 2011, where she shares her own gardening experiences and interviews with gardening experts. In 2017, she learned more about the seed industry and edibles tailored to the home gardener when she visited the California Vegetable Trials, through a National Garden Bureau sponsorship. She has been a guest on several gardening podcasts. *Micro Food Gardening* is her first book.

# AUTHOR ACKNOWLEDGMENTS

Several people have made this book possible—and what a wonderful journey it has been.

Thank you to my husband Rob, who entertained all my spur-of-the-moment ideas for garden projects that would happen in the middle of dinner, midway through conversations, or just as he was about to nod off to sleep. Thanks for living with all the tiny plants. Actually, thanks for living with all of my plants—indoors and outdoors.

I am grateful to the Cool Springs Press and Quarto Publishing team—Jessica Walliser, Regina Grenier, Anne Re, Nyle Vialet, John Gettings, Marilyn Kecyk, Steve Roth, and others who have contributed to the book you are holding in your hands.

Thanks to my family and friends for their support—and sometimes the use of their homes as backdrops for several micro food projects: Del and Bob McGuinness, Tricia Ackerman, and Kelle Young. Kelle also agreed to model and demonstrate how to build some of the projects in this book, along with my friend Amanda Arce—thank you both for agreeing to stay when I showed up with a carload of supplies. And speaking of building projects, thanks to Bob for consulting on my project ideas and helping me build my prototype rain barrel. (It didn't leak!)

Thanks to my Dad, Bernard Haggerty, who enabled me as a child to be a gardener and encouraged me to grow each and every tomato. Thank you to the National Garden Bureau—Diane Blazek and Gail Pabst—for sponsoring me as an NGB Plant Nerd for a week of learning and adventure during the Veggie Trials tour. I not only met amazing people passionate about growing food, but it opened my eyes to the varieties available to the home gardener.

Thanks to Angie Lituri, my BFF, who is always supportive, positive and understands the fear that groundhogs can cause when they get too close to my plants. Thank you to Katherine Hunter and Jess Graham, who would encourage me to keep writing throughout the long weekends and always seem to know the right thing to say.

Thank you to the readers of Frau Zinnie and for those who follow me on my social media handles. I love talking about gardening with you.

If you want it, you can grow it. Let's keep growing, friends.

# INDEX

## K

kale (*Brassica napus*), for sprouting, 147
kale (*Brassica oleracea*)
    caterpillars eating, 41, 133
    for Cool Cookie Container Combo, 137
    for Edible Side Table, 38, 40, 41
    growing tips for, 133
    in head planters, 124
    as microgreen seed, 155
    for Omelet Combo, 142
kitchen items, as containers, 20
kohlrabi (*Brassica oleracea*), 155

## L

leafy greens, lighting needs of, 23
lemon basil (*Ocimum americanum*), 159
lettuce (*Lactuca sativa*)
    cut-and-come-again, 16
    for Edible Side Table, 38, 40, 41
    growing tips for, 35
    harvesting and succession sowing, 36
    for Lettuce Bicycle Basket, 32
    for Micro Food Fountain, 77
Lettuce Bicycle Basket, 32–36
lettuce leaf basil (*Ocimum basilicum* 'Lettuce Leaf'), 159
lighting, 21–23
Living Wreath, Rainwater Collector with, 104–10

## M

mason jars, 6
    for Omelet Combo, 138–40

for Windowsill Pea Shoots, 160–62
Melon Magic Trellis, 94–98
melons (*Cucumis melo*), 14, 26, 95, 97, 98
metal containers, 19
metal shelving, for two-tier grow light area, 151
micro edibles
    benefits of growing, 9
    containers for (*see* containers)
    defined, 8
    drainage for, 25
    factors in choosing, 165
    fertilizers for, 25, 27, 28–29, 92
    grown from seed, 8, 9, 13–16
    hardening off, 16, 78, 85
    lighting for, 21–23
    soil for, 26–27
    sources of, 8, 13, 17
    watering, 24–25, 92
Micro Food Fountain, 74–78
micro food gardening
    benefits of, 9
    for limited space, 7
    locations for, 10–13
microgreen seeds, 155
Microgreens project, 152–55
Mini Salsa Garden, 115–17
Mini Stir-Fry Garden, 62–67
Mint (*Mentha* spp.), 124
mirasol chile pepper (*Capsicum annuum*), 90
Muffin Pan Basil, 156–59
muffin pans
    for Muffin Pan Basil, 156, 157–58
    starting seedlings in, 20
mung bean (*Vigna radiata*), for sprouting, 147
mustard (*Brassica juncea*), 136, 137, 147, 155

## N

nasturtiums (*Tropaeolum minus*)
    as edible flowers, 59, 60, 61
    in head planters, 124
    in Micro Food Fountain, 75, 77
newspaper pots, for seed starting, 15
nitrogen (N), in fertilizer, 28, 29

## O

Omelet Combo, 138–42
oregano (*Origanum vulgare*), 59, 91
organic edible flowers, 58
organic fertilizers, 25, 27, 28–29
organic soil blends, 27
ornamental plants, defined, 8
outdoor projects
    Baby Bok Choy Cups, 48–51
    Basket Root Garden, 68–69
    Cherry Tomato Candy, 118–21
    Cool Cookie Container Combo, 134–37
    Cuke Tower, 111–14
    Edible Flowers, 57–61
    Edible Side Table, 37–41
    Fingerling Potato Window Box, 52–56
    Hanging Gutter Garden, 42–47
    It's All in Your Head, 122–25
    Lettuce Bicycle Basket, 32–36
    Melon Magic Trellis, 94–98
    Micro Food Fountain, 74–78
    Mini Salsa Garden, 115–17
    Rainwater Collector with Living Wreath, 104–10
    Repurposed Aquarium, 79–81
    Shady Garden Bed, 130–33